about the house

GCSE edition

Helen McGrath

Oxford University Press 1987

Oxford University Press, Walton Street, Oxford OX2 6DP

Oxford   New York   Toronto
Delhi   Bombay   Calcutta   Madras   Karachi
Petaling Jaya   Singapore   Hong Kong   Tokyo
Nairobi   Dar es Salaam   Cape Town
Melbourne   Auckland

and associated companies in
Beirut   Berlin   Ibadan   Nicosia

Oxford is a trade mark of Oxford University Press

© Oxford University Press 1987

First published 1980
Second edition 1987
ISBN 0 19 832754 4

Acknowledgements

Illustrations are by Patricia Capon, Marion Mills and Lynne Willey.
The back cover illustration is by Stephen Cocking.

The publishers would like to thank the following for permission to reproduce
photographs:

Albright and Wilson Ltd. p.40; Barnaby's Picture Library; Camera Press;
Format Photographers Ltd./Brenda Price p.218; Sally and Richard Greenhill
p.165; Job Centre, Oxford p.212; Rob Judges p.16, p.19, p.23, p.167, p.205;
Thames Water Authority (Vales Division); UB 40, Oxford/P. Massie p.219;
Universal Pictorial Press and Agency Ltd p 151.

The publishers would like to thank the Consumers' Association for permission
to reproduce the extract from *Which?* on p. 162.

Set by Tradespools Ltd., Frome, Somerset
Printed by Cambridge University Press

Preface

About the house has been completely updated and revised to take account of changes and developments in areas relating to the home and family. New topics introduced include food additives, food labelling regulations, Housing Associations, house purchase through shared ownership, the purchase of council houses, sheltered accommodation, different types of mortgages, Building Society accounts as an alternative to bank accounts, department store credit accounts, budgeting for household bills, conserving energy in homes, developments in fitted kitchens, cookers and microwave ovens, the A.S.A. (Advertising Standards Authority), the new system of D.H.S.S. benefits, current government training schemes including Youth Training Schemes and job creation schemes of different kinds, new qualifications from Colleges of Further Education.

Recent developments in examination syllabuses have brought a change of emphasis to the curriculum. The emphasis is less on mastering and committing to memory an ever-growing syllabus content and more on helping pupils to acquire reasoning skills which they can transfer from one situation to another. Based on information they have acquired, pupils are encouraged to consider any given problem, to investigate different ways of solving it, and to decide on the most suitable decision or appropriate course of action.

If pupils are given time to consider and reflect on the knowledge they acquire and to learn to communicate it and apply it, it is hoped that they will develop skills of reasoning and decision-making which they can then apply to any sort of problem.

In this book, the content and subject matter relating to the home economics syllabus is provided in the body of the chapters. At the end of each chapter is a series of suggestions for investigations by pupils which put the pupil into the role of decision-maker. Problems are posed in matters which relate to pupils and their families as closely as possible. Pupils may then investigate possible solutions, come to a conclusion or decision, and work out how to implement it. There can be a subsequent evaluation of how well the problem has been resolved.

Suggestions for investigative work vary in complexity but the open-ended nature of the tasks set will allow pupils of widely varying abilities to approach them. All pupils can be expected to consider the problem at some level, while there is scope for certain pupils to carry out a thorough and carefully reasoned study.

There is no implication that these tasks are to be subjects of written work only. It is hoped that they will suggest topics for discussion, in groups or as a class, for role-play, or for individual project work, at the discretion of the teacher.

Contents

Chapter 1

Choosing a home

Finding a home

Many different kinds of housing are available in this country. They include not only houses but bungalows, flats, bedsits, lodgings, hostels, and sheltered accommodation. People's needs change as they go through different stages in their lives. Some accommodation would suit young people who have just left home to live on their own, while other kinds may be more suitable for young married couples or elderly people. Larger families with children, perhaps with relatives living with them, have other housing needs.

Though people's houses may be very different, they all have things in common which make them home for those who live in them. They provide:

shelter from the weather (storms, rain, snow)
warmth
safety from other people
a meeting place for the family
a familiar place where you belong and feel comfortable

These are the things that make a place feel 'homely', not how thick the carpets are, nor how smart the furniture is, nor how large the television.

Choosing a home

Choosing a home is an important step. You may be living there for several years so you should think carefully about what you want before you decide. The cost is usually the main consideration; you work out what you can afford and then see what is available at that price. Whether you plan to rent or buy, there are several points to consider when you are looking at flats or houses.

The environment
1 *The area* Is it in a pleasant neighbourhood, with gardens, trees, open spaces, and well-kept houses, or is it affected by vandalism, litter, and decaying property?
2 *Employment* Is it reasonably near to the place where you work, or will you have to spend a lot of time and money on travelling?
3 *Transport* Are there good buses, trains, and roads for you to get to work or school and to go out?
4 *Shopping* Are there good shops nearby?
5 *Services* Are there schools, doctors, and a library nearby?
6 *Entertainment* Are leisure facilities available for people of different ages, e.g. youth club, sports centre, cinema, park, swimming pool?
7 You may not wish to be too close to a sewage works, canal, main road, airport, nuclear power station, etc.

The house or flat itself
1 *Cost* You will not only have to consider the cost of rent or mortgage, but rates, water rates, heating bills, insurance of the building and contents, necessary transport to work or school, maintenance.
2 *Size* You need enough room for the number of people who are to live there, but it should not be so large that it is expensive to maintain, furnish, decorate, and keep warm.

3   *Central heating* Most people want central heating to keep comfortably warm at a reasonable cost and to provide hot water (see page 66).

4   *Insulation* If the house is well insulated, fuel bills will be lower and you will feel more comfortable (see page 58). You may be able to get a grant towards the cost of insulating the roof.

5   *Electrical wiring* A modern system with 13 amp sockets is safest and most useful. It is expensive to have a house rewired.

6   *Aspect* If the windows face south or west the house will have more sun and will feel brighter and warmer than if it faces north or east.

7   *A garden* You may like gardening or you may not want to spend the hours needed to keep a garden tidy.

8   *Storage space* Plenty of cupboards and fitted wardrobes are very useful. They help keep the house tidy and save you buying freestanding cupboards.

9   *Eating* Is there an eating area in the kitchen, or is the dining area in the living room? There may be a separate dining room which could also be used as a quiet room for work or study.

10   *Fittings* Is the house ready to move into? Does it need a lot of work and money to improve it? Are fitted carpets and curtains included with the house?

Questions

1   **What is the difference between a house and a home?**
2   **Make a list of all the good and bad points you would look out for in an area you were thinking of moving into.**
3   **What do you consider the six most important points to look for when choosing a house? Say why each is important.**

Types of housing available

Houses

Houses may be detached (standing on their own in a garden) or semi-detached (one of two joined together). Several houses joined together are called terraced houses; modern homes joined in a row like this are called town houses or link houses. Houses are usually larger than flats, so may be more suitable for larger families and those with children. Children can play outside a house in the garden or yard without being far from their parents. It is easy to hang washing outside and to take out rubbish. You are more likely to get to know your neighbours than if you live in a flat.

Bungalows

Bungalows are houses, detached or semi-detached with all the rooms on the ground floor. There is no upper floor. Elderly or handicapped people often prefer bungalows as there are no stairs to climb. Bungalows may be more expensive as they take up more land. They may cost more to keep warm if there are more outside walls exposed to the cold.

Flats

Flats are usually smaller than houses and have all the rooms on one level. Owing to their small size they are often cheaper to buy or rent, and to decorate, furnish, and keep warm. You do not have to maintain the outside or the shared areas of the building yourself, although you may have to pay a charge for this to be done. Flats can make good and convenient homes for single people and couples without young children. For those with small children they may be less suitable. There is not much room inside the flat where children can play and it is impossible for a parent to watch over young children playing outside from several floors up. It is difficult to carry up the push-chairs, prams, washing, and shopping, especially when the lift is out of order. It can be lonely too, as people do not meet on the doorstep or in the garden, giving them a chance to chat with neighbours and become friendly with them.

Sharing a flat

Sharing with friends means that you have the company of other young people and you share costs. The only trouble here is that arguments can easily arise about shared jobs like cleaning, cooking, or washing up. Sometimes it is difficult to share costs fairly. One person may use more heat and hot water, eat more food, or make more telephone calls than the others, and this can cause resentment if everyone is paying an equal amount.

Uniflats or studio flats

These can provide suitable small homes for sale to single people or couples without children. They consist of one large room with a kitchen and bathroom area. They often come fully decorated, carpeted, and fitted with a washing machine/drier, refrigerator, fold-down bed, table, and so on. This means that the person buying does not have to find extra money for these items; they are all included in the monthly mortgage repayments.

Bedsitting-rooms

These are rooms to rent from private landlords, usually in a large older house. Each person has his/her own combined bedroom/living room, but often the bathroom and kitchen have to be shared with other people in the house. This is often the cheapest kind of accommodation and can be suitable for single people, but would be inconvenient for a family with children.

ABINGDON, fourth person to share house, small room, central heating, parking. — Tel. Bicester 25305   96564

BEDSIT, own cooking and washing facilities; Headington area; £29 pw, inclusive. — Oxford 6286   95993

PERSON REQUIRED for friendly shared house in Oxford, close to centre, £105 pcm, plus share of bills. — Tel. Oxford 24899   99657

PROFESSIONAL PERSON (female preferred), shared house, Eynsham; £120 pcm plus bills. — Oxford 88062   13488

ROOM AVAILABLE in modern Semi, all mod cons, Oxford 3 miles, £30 per week, inclusive. — Tel. Kidlington 7191 evenings.   99626

ROOM TO LET off Cumnor Hill, share kitchen, bathroom with 2 others. — Tel. Oxford 86249   96541

SINGLE ROOM in large flat, £40 per week inclusive, use of kitchen and bathroom, working person only. — Tel. Oxford 72551   99544

WOODSTOCK. — Own Room in 2-bedroomed flat to let, to share all facilities, £135 pcm, plus bills, non-smoker preferred. — Tel. Woodstock 81340 weekends or evenings, or Oxford 5773 weekdays.   94999

Lodgings

You can look in the paper for advertisements for board and lodgings. The owner cooks meals, keeps your room clean, and provides and washes sheets and pillowcases. This has several advantages. It saves you the trouble of cooking, cleaning, and shopping for food, and makes sure (if the owner is a good cook) that you are well fed. You usually have the company of other people in the house.

However, you will probably pay more each week and be less independent than if you were in your own flat. You will be less able to please yourself about the hours at which you come in and go out, and the friends who come to visit you and how long they stay.

Hostels

Some towns and cities have hostels for young people, such as the YMCA and YWCA. If you can get a place in a hostel, which is not always easy, you will be provided with a room, heating, hot water, and hot meals, plus the company of others. Charges are fairly high, but everything you need is provided. You can find out about hostels in any area by inquiring at the Citizens' Advice Bureau, or sometimes the local library.

Colleges and universities often have hostels or halls of residence where their own students can live. There is usually an accommodation officer to help students find a place to live.

Sheltered accommodation

This is for elderly or handicapped people and gives them independence together with a certain amount of care and supervision. Some homes of this kind are available for sale, while others can be rented from the local authority or a housing association.

An elderly person or couple has a room or flatlet which can often be furnished with their own belongings if they wish, so that they have familiar possessions around them.

There are several rooms or flatlets together with a live-in warden who can be called by a buzzer if the old person needs help at any time. There may be a shared living room so that residents can have the company of others when they feel like it. Some hot meals may be provided, which helps keep old people in good health when they do not feel like cooking for one. Usually the buildings are specially built or adapted so that, for example, light switches and sockets are easy to reach, there are handrails in toilets and bathrooms, lifts to floors above ground level, and doors wide enough for wheelchairs.

Renting privately

Bedsitting rooms, flats, and houses can be rented from a private landlord as well as from the council or corporation. They may be furnished or unfurnished and the rent is usually higher than council rent. If you feel that the rent is unfairly high for the property you can ask the Rent Officer from the local Housing Department to set a fair rent which the landlord cannot increase.

Tenants of privately rented flats and rooms now have quite a lot of protection under the law against harassment or eviction by the landlord. In return they are expected to pay their rent, keep the property in good order, and to act reasonably. Disagreements between landlords and tenants may be referred to the Local Authority's Rent Tribunal to be sorted out.

Date	Rent Due	Date	Cash Received	Arrears	By whom Received
					P. Jones
16 June	£135 00	16 June	£135 00		P. Jones
23 June	£135 00	23 June	£135 00		P. Jones
30 June	£135 00	30 June	£135 00		P. Jones
7 July	£135 00	7 July	£135 00		P. Jones
	£125 00	14 July	£135 00		P. Jones

All tenants, whether council or private, should be given a rent book by the landlord with details of the rent and the tenant's legal rights. It should show the name and address of both landlord and tenant. It is important that it is filled in, dated, and signed every time rent is paid, as proof of payment.

Housing benefit is available, as with council housing, to help those on a low income to pay their rent and rates.

TO LET

BOTLEY, 2 bedroom family House, 1 year	**£350 pcm**
BERINSFIELD, 2 bedroom family House, 1 year	**£340 pcm**
KIDLINGTON, 3 bed family House, 1 year	**£420 pcm**
SOUTHMOOR, 3 bedroom family House, 1 year	**£450 pcm**
WOOTTEN, 4 bedroom family House, 5 months	**£650 pcm**
WOODSTOCK, 3 bedroom family House, 1 year	**£350 pcm**
KENNINGTON, 3 bedroom family/ shared House, 1 year	**£450 pcm**
N. OXFORD, 4 bedroom family House, 5 months	**£700 pcm**

DIDCOT, three-bedroomed furnished semi-detached Cottage in exceptional condition, gas central heating, telephone, parking space, £295 pcm, available mid May. For further details and viewing. — Tel. Didcot 81218   96662

SEMI TO LET, 3 bedroomed, Cowley area. — Tel. Oxford 6077, after 8 p.m.   95009

SUMMERTOWN, luxuriously appointed large two double-bedroomed Flat, dining room or study, sitting room, kitchen / breakfast, garage and gardens, available immediately for up to one year, references, deposit required, rental £530 monthly, inclusive of rates. — Tel. Oxford 51530   963732

THREE-BEDROOMED fully furnished House to let, Marsden area, superb condition, sharers or family. — Tel. 0869 4053, or Oxford 95731 evenings only.   96531

EAST OXFORD

Self-contained two bedroomed Flat, furnished, fully carpeted, TV, telephone, fridge/freezer, suit professional couple, minimum one year lease. References required.

£300 pcm

Tel:
Oxford 24190

Sharers Considered
Grove – Modern fully equipped three bedroom house, available now. £295.00 pcm

Finding privately rented accommodation

The best source is the 'Flats to let' column of the local paper, or you could advertise in the 'Flats wanted' column. Accommodation agencies often advertise there too, but the tenant sometimes has to pay a fee to the agency. Newsagents shops may have postcards in their windows showing rooms and flats to rent in that area.

Questions

1   **Name four kinds of accommodation suitable for someone leaving home for the first time.**
2   **Give three advantages and three disadvantages of sharing a flat with friends.**
3   **How would you find lodgings in a town you did not know?**
4   **List the services you would expect to find in lodgings.**
5   **What are the drawbacks of living in lodgings?**
6   **List points for and against living in a hostel.**
7   **What kind of accommodation would suit:**
    a   An apprentice on a training course for three months?
    b   a girl going to college in a town where she did not know anyone?
    c   a young couple moving into a town for one year, while one partner was studying?
8   **How would you start to look for a furnished flat?**
9   **Where would you apply for Housing Benefit to help pay rent and/or rates?**
10   **Describe the advantages of sheltered accommodation for an elderly person.**

Buying a home

There are several advantages in buying a home of your own if you can. This is usually done by saving up the deposit, then making monthly mortgage payments over about twenty five years until the house is paid for.

Advantages of buying rather than renting

1   Depending on what you can afford, you have more choice where you live than if you were housed by the council.
2   If you make improvements to the house (such as installing central heating or new windows) you will increase the value of the house for when you sell it. If you spend money to improve a council or landlord's property you never get your money back. You do, however, have the right to buy your council home.
    If you are buying your own house or flat you do not need to ask the council's permission to make alterations (though you do need planning permission for major alterations like an extension or a garage in the garden).
4   If you move, you can usually sell the property for more than you paid for it, as most houses go up in value over the years.
5   You can sell up and move on fairly easily.
6   Once your house is paid for (though it may take 25 years to do so), it belongs to you. When you are old and have a lower income you will not have further payments to make. You can leave your house to your family in your will.
7   If you would like to buy a home of your own but can't quite afford to, 'shared ownership schemes' make it easier. (Page 21 shows you how this works.)

Some disadvantages of buying rather than renting

1   You have to save up for the deposit and then pay all the fees involved in buying (see page 20).
2   You have to pay the costs of all repairs to the property.
3   You have to pay general and water rates as well as the mortgage. Council tenants usually have one payment only which includes rates.

Starting to look for a home to buy

Before you start to look seriously you need to know how much you can afford to pay. On the next page you will see how this is worked out. Once you know the sort of price you can afford you could:

1   Visit estate agents and ask if they have anything suitable for you. They help people to buy and sell property by advertising it in their own windows and in newspapers and by putting up 'For Sale' boards outside the house. If they sell a house they charge the seller (or vendor) a fee of about 1–2% of the price.
2   Look in the area in which you would like to live for 'For Sale' boards.
3   Look in the 'Property for sale' columns in your local paper.

Some advertisements use these terms:
Starter homes or 'ideal for first time buyer'. This just means that they are a reasonable price and size.
Freehold You own the house and the land it is built on.
Leasehold You do not own the land the house is built on. You have to pay ground rent and/or a service charge for it. Flats are usually leasehold and this money is partly used to cover the upkeep of shared corridors, lifts, gardens, and so on.
Semi Semi-detached.
Tce. Terrace.
Sep. w.c. Separate water closet (toilet) i.e. not in the bathroom.
Col. suite Coloured (not white) bath, toilet, and washbasin.
Rec. Reception room i.e. a living room.
F 'robes. Fitted wardrobes.
V.P. Vacant possession means that the house will be vacant for you to move into as soon as the sale is completed.
C.H. Central heating.
O.N.O. Or near offer.

Questions

1   **What are the three main advantages of buying a house rather than renting one?**
2   **Cut some 'Property for sale' columns out of your local paper and explain any abbreviations in them. See if you can find the average cost of:**
    a a three-bedroomed semi in your area
    b a three-bedroomed terrace house
    c a four-bedroomed detached house
    d a two-bedroomed bungalow

Paying for the house

Very few people can raise the money to buy a house outright. Most people arrange a mortgage. This is a loan which is paid off in monthly instalments over a long period of time – usually about 25 years.

Where can you obtain a mortgage?

Building Societies are the most common source.

Banks Most banks, including the TSB, lend money to buy homes.

Insurance companies may arrange endowment mortgages (see below).

Local authorities sometimes lend money, especially to buy older properties within their own area. They are more willing to lend to low wage earners. They must offer mortgages to tenants wanting to buy their own council homes.

Mortgage brokers can help you obtain a mortgage. They will look at the different types and sources available and will find one suitable for your circumstances. This can be useful if you are having difficulty in getting a loan. You are not charged anything for this service.

How the mortgage system works

1 You can usually borrow about 90% of the value of the house and you have to put down the other 10% as a deposit. On a few properties you can get 100% mortgage if you have a very reliable income.
2 You should save regularly with a bank or building society for the deposit. Then they are likely to lend you money for the mortage.
3 You pay back a regular monthly sum over the 25-year period. You do not own the house until it is completely paid for.
4 Different types of mortgage are available. Details are given on page 20.

Asking for a loan

A bank or building society will lend you money if they think you will be able to pay them back.
1 They will check whether you have a steady income.
2 They will lend you 2½–3 times your yearly wage or salary.
3 Single people and couples can apply for a mortgage. In the case of a couple, both salaries can be taken into account when decisions are made about the amount of the loan. It has to be considered that one of the partners may stop working if they have children.
4 First time buyers will be considered favourably for a loan.
5 Building societies and banks will check the value and condition of the house before they will lend you money to buy it. They do this by getting a valuer's report on it. You have to pay for this.
6 When you start thinking of looking for a home to buy, it is a good idea to visit a bank or building society. You can discuss your income with them and find out how much they would be willing to lend you (on a suitable property). They can give you a mortgage certificate stating this, so that when you find the right place you can make an offer to buy it without then having to find out how much you can borrow.

Surveyor

When you have found a house that seems suitable you can consider whether to pay a surveyor to give you a detailed report on the structure of the house. He/she will look at the roof, walls, floors, and so on for any signs of rot, woodworm, cracks, damp, and any other faults.

He/she should point out any expensive repairs that may be needed. This is more important in an old house. You have to pay for the survey, but if faults are found you may be able to get the house for a lower price.

National House Building Council

New houses can be issued with a certificate from the NHBC if they are built to a high standard. They will pay compensation if any faults develop in the first two years. After two years they will pay only for *major* repairs, such as a new roof. Look for this certificate if buying any house up to 10 years old.

Solicitor

You will need a solicitor to carry out the legal side of buying your home. You should ask several for a quotation, as costs vary a lot from one to another for the same work. Some builders of new houses and flats will pay your legal fees, especially for first time buyers.

Questions
1 **What percentage of the price of a new house can you usually borrow from a Building Society or bank?**
2 **How should you save for the deposit on a house?**
3 **How long does it usually take to pay off the mortgage on a house?**
4 **What is a mortgage and how often do you make repayments?**
5 **What information do Building Societies require before they decide whether to lend money?**
6 **How much could you expect to borrow if you earned £6000 a year?**
7 **You are thinking of buying a house built five years ago. How could a NHBC certificate help you?**

Costs of buying

Summary of the costs you may have when buying:

The deposit
Cost of valuer's report
Surveyor's fees
Solicitor's fees
Insurance of the house and contents
If you are selling one house to buy another you might also have estate agent's fees and furniture removal costs.

Government grants may be available for improving older houses which do not have the basic amenities of an indoor WC, bath or shower, sink, washbasin, hot and cold water supply, or for major repairs to the structure of the house. Your local council has details of these.

Mortgages

There are two main types of mortgages available. You would discuss with the building society which would be better for you.

Repayment mortgage

The loan is paid over the agreed time, e.g. 25 years, in monthly instalments. Each payment includes both some of the capital sum you borrowed and the interest due on it.

If the person paying the mortage has a dependent family, he or she should take out insurance so that if he or she dies, the mortgage is fully paid off and the family owns the house without needing to make any further payments. This insurance adds a small extra monthly cost to the mortgage repayments.

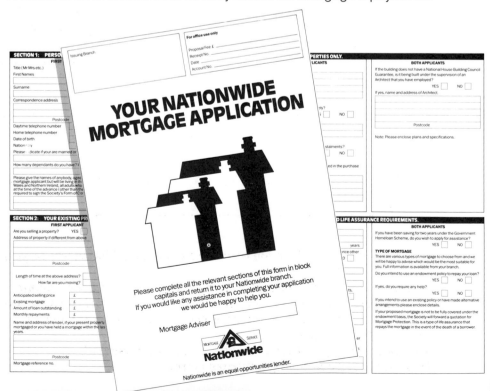

Endowment mortgage

This costs more each month but at the end of the 25 years you receive a lump sum. (It is really a way of saving.) You could choose a low-cost endowment policy where monthly repayments are less but any lump sum you get is much smaller. Endowment policies give you built-in insurance. If the person paying the mortgage dies, the loan is paid off and the dependent family owns the home.

Each month you pay a premium to the insurance company and some interest on the loan to the building society. At the end of the 25 years the insurance company pays off the capital sum you owe and the house is yours.

Housing Associations

These are non-profit-making organizations. They provide houses and flats at reasonable prices to people in need of housing. They receive government funds to enable them to do this. They may build new houses and flats, or they may renovate older properties to a good standard and convert them into several self-contained flats.

Some associations may sell or let their homes only to certain groups of people, perhaps only to the elderly, or only to single people of working age. These are often people who would have so few points on a council waiting list that they would have little chance of being housed by the council.

Associations can provide houses and flats for people to rent or buy. Where they provide homes for sale, they must be within a reasonable price range. They are sold through special low-cost home ownership schemes to people who could not otherwise afford to buy.

These schemes include:

a   *Shared ownership* for people who cannot afford to buy a home outright. You buy a share of the property and pay rent on the remainder. This makes your monthly payment less. In a few years' time, when your income is likely to have gone up, you can if you wish buy further shares in your home until it is eventually all yours. Your rent goes down as you buy more.

b   *Leasehold schemes* for the elderly. This enables elderly people to buy a sheltered home on a long lease at about 70% of its normal cost.

The government has set up a Housing Corporation which encourages and supervises the many housing associations in Britain. (There are about 2600 of them.) They provide about half a million homes to rent and for sale, for people who need them.

You should be able to get the address of their office in your area from your local Housing Advice Centre, Citizens' Advice Bureau, or council offices.

Questions

1   **You are buying your first flat which is newly built. What costs do you expect to have?**
2   **You have a young family and are buying a house with a repayment mortgage. How could you ensure that it would be paid for if you were to die?**
3   **Why does an endowment mortgage cost more each month than a repayment mortgage?**
4   **Who is likely to get a home through a Housing Association?**
5   **How do shared ownership schemes work?**

Renting a home from the council

Most rented houses and flats in this country are rented from local councils. The council is your <u>landlord</u> and you are the <u>tenant</u>. There are certain advantages in being a council tenant and renting rather than buying.

1   The council carries out and pays for all necessary repairs.
2   They pay for modernizations such as rewiring or installing central heating, though you may have to pay a higher rent afterwards.
3   You do not have to save a large deposit as you often have to if you want to buy your own home.
4   You have the right to buy your council home after renting it for two years (see below).
5   You can receive housing benefit to help pay rent and rates, depending upon your income and your expenses. People who are buying their home may get help in paying their rates.

Disadvantages of living in rented property

1   You pay rent all your life and your home never belongs to you.
2   You have restricted choice about the house and the area it is in.
3   You cannot make alterations without permission.
4   You may have to wait a long time for repairs to be done.
5   It can be difficult to exchange houses if you want to move.
6   You may have a long wait on the council list.

The council housing waiting list

To apply for a council-owned house or flat you must put your name on the waiting list. You may have to wait from a couple of weeks to several years to be housed. The Housing Officer has to decide in a fair way who is in most urgent need of a house. People are usually awarded points, according to the conditions they now live under. The people with the most points go to the top of the list and are rehoused first. These are the kind of conditions you are given points for:

Overcrowding in your present home
Sharing a kitchen or bath with another family
Having no bath, inside toilet, or hot water
Being homeless, particularly if you have children
If you leave a house that is tied to a job, e.g. school caretaker
Medical reasons e.g. if you live on the third floor and have asthma
If you have young children in a high-rise flat
If you live in a home too large for you
If you have been on the list a long time

Your right to buy your house

Most council and new-town tenants have a legal right to buy their home if they wish to, provided they have lived in it for at least two years. Depending upon how long you have lived in and paid rent for your home, you are entitled to buy it at a discount price. You have the right to a mortgage from your council if you want it. You are entitled to 100% mortgage from them, provided your income is

high enough. You can also choose to part buy, part rent your home through a shared ownership scheme (see page 21).

Advice on housing

You can obtain leaflets about these and other aspects of housing from the Housing Department you pay your rent to, from Housing Advice Centres in cities, from the Citizens Advice Bureau, and from the Department of the Environment Regional Office (look up their address in your local phone book).

Questions

1 **Who owns council houses and flats?**
2 **What is a council tenant?**
3 **What do you think are the two main advantages of living in council property?**
4 **What do you think are the two main disadvantages of living in council property?**
5 **If you wanted to apply for housing benefit, where would you go for information on how to do this?**
6 **If you were a council tenant, what reasons could there be for and against buying your home?**

Rates

Who pays rates?

Every householder (i.e. one person in the house or flat) has to pay rates. If you live in a home rented from the council your rates are usually paid along with your rent. If you are buying a home you have to pay rates as well as the mortgage.

What are the rates used for?

The rates collected by the local authority or council are used to pay for local services for all the people in the area. These include:

Police, fire and civil defence
Local transport services
Education, libraries, parks, museums, leisure centres, swimming pools
Housing, social services, refuse collection
Consumer advice centres

How much do you pay?

The amount you pay depends on two things:

1   The rateable value of your house. The rateable value depends on the value of your house. The more amenities it has (size, gardens, pleasant area, garage), the higher the rateable value and the more you pay in rates. The rateable value of the house shown opposite is £218.

2   Each year the local council sets a rate in the pound to be charged. For example, if one year the council sets the rate in the pound at £3, then you would pay the rateable value of your house (£218) × the rate in the pound (£3). So you would pay £218 × 3
$$= £654 \text{ for the year.}$$

In the rate demand shown opposite, the rate in the pound for the area is £2.733. The rateable value of the house is £218, so the amount you would have to pay would be £218 × 2.733
$$= £595.79 \text{ for the year.}$$

How do you pay?

You can pay:
a all at once
b in two instalments
c in ten equal monthly instalments (so each one is about £59 for each of ten months).

Housing Benefit

If you have only an average or low income you can apply for a rate rebate from your local council. The amount you pay is reduced according to your income and your family expenses.

Water Rates

Householders have to pay water rates as well as general rates. Sometimes the cost is included with the general rates, sometimes it is in a separate bill. It is used to provide a clean water supply, for sewage disposal, control of water pollution, and recreation and nature conservancy on rivers, lakes, and reservoirs.

Questions

1 **Who has to pay rates?**
2 **How do council tenants pay their rates?**
3 **How often do you pay rates if you are buying your own home?**
4 **List some of the more important services to the community which are paid for by the rates.**
5 **The rateable value of your house is £240. The rates are 90p in the pound. How much will your yearly rates bill be? How much would you have to pay each month?**
6 **The rateable value of your house is £200. The rates are £2.20 in the pound. How much will your yearly rates bill be?**
7 **Who can apply for housing benefit to help pay rates?**

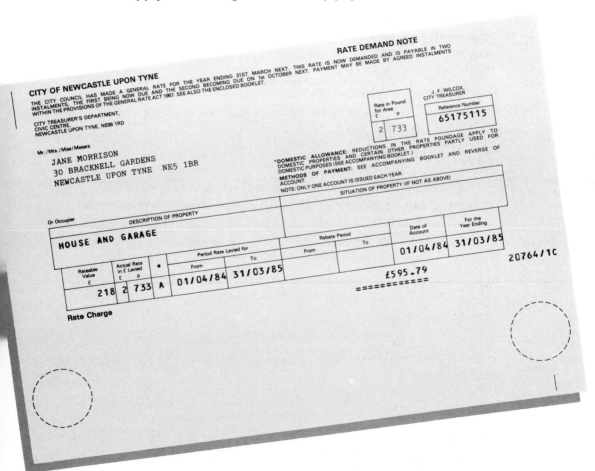

RATE DEMAND NOTE

THIS RATE IS NOW DEMANDED AND IS PAYABLE IN TWO INSTALMENTS
PAYMENT MAY BE MADE BY AGREED

CITY OF NEWCASTLE UPON TYNE

THE CITY COUNCIL HAS MADE A GENERAL RATE FOR THE YEAR ENDING 31ST MARCH NEXT. INSTALMENTS, THE FIRST BEING NOW DUE AND THE SECOND BECOMING DUE ON 1st OCTOBER NEXT. WITHIN THE PROVISIONS OF THE GENERAL RATE ACT 1967. SEE ALSO THE ENCLOSED BOOKLET.

CITY TREASURER'S DEPARTMENT,
CIVIC CENTRE,
NEWCASTLE UPON TYNE, NE99 1RD

J. F. WILCOX,
CITY TREASURER

Rate in Pound for Area	
£	p
2	733

Reference Number
65175115

Mr./Mrs./Miss/Messrs
JANE MORRISON
30 BRACKNELL GARDENS
NEWCASTLE UPON TYNE   NE5 1BR

*DOMESTIC ALLOWANCE: REDUCTIONS IN THE RATE POUNDAGE APPLY TO DOMESTIC PROPERTIES AND CERTAIN OTHER PROPERTIES PARTLY USED FOR DOMESTIC PURPOSES (SEE ACCOMPANYING BOOKLET.)
METHODS OF PAYMENT: SEE ACCOMPANYING BOOKLET AND REVERSE OF ACCOUNT.
NOTE: ONLY ONE ACCOUNT IS ISSUED EACH YEAR.
SITUATION OF PROPERTY (IF NOT AS ABOVE)

Or Occupier   DESCRIPTION OF PROPERTY

HOUSE AND GARAGE

Rateable Value £	Actual Rate in £ Levied £ p	*	Period Rate Levied for From	To	Rebate Period From	To	Date of Account	For the Year Ending
218	2 733	A	01/04/84	31/03/85			01/04/84	31/03/85

£595·79
=============

20764/1C

Rate Charge

Further work on chapter 1

1   Have a look around your local shopping area and see how many names of different estate agents, building societies, and banks you can collect. You may be surprised at how many there are.

2   Your parents have agreed to your leaving home to share a flat with a friend. Find out what is available in your area.

3   A couple who are friends of yours are wondering whether to rent or to buy a flat. They both have full-time jobs. What information can you give them to help them decide?

4   You earn £7000 a year and are saving up to buy a flat. Find out what is available in your price range in the area where you live.

5   Being homeless or living in poor housing conditions is very distressing. Find out what you can about the situation of homeless people.

Sources of further information

Housing Advice Centres in cities, Housing Department of your local council, Department of Environment Regional Offices, Citizens' Advice Bureaux (all addresses in your local phone book).

Newspaper advertisements, free newspapers from estate agents, show houses.

You can write to the following (enclosing a stamped addressed envelope) for a list of informative booklets, which are often free:

Shelter: National Campaign for the Homeless, 157 Waterloo Road, London SE1 8XF.

Shac (The London Housing Aid Centre), 189a Old Brompton Road, London SW5.

The Building Societies Association, 3 Savile Row, London W1X 1AF.

The Housing Corporation, 149 Tottenham Court Road, London W1P 0BN.

Community Service Volunteers, 237 Pentonville Road, London N1 9NJ, have leaflets, games, etc. on the family, community, disability, poverty, housing, old age, personal relationships, unemployment, and so on.

Halifax Building Society, PO Box 60, Trinity Road, Halifax, West Yorks (or local offices) have free booklets on housing and home management, etc.

Computer software
Walcam Ltd., 23 Deansgate Lane, Timperley, Cheshire WA15 6SF. Cassettes and discs, BBC, 'Choosing a Home' and 'Buying a Home'.

Book
Things you need to know by Pen Keyte, Oxford University Press.

Chapter 2

Services to the home

Natural gas

Gas is an important domestic fuel in Britain, providing energy for warmth, hot water, and cooking to about 16 million homes. It is by far the most widely-used fuel in British homes, providing more heat than electricity, solid fuel, and oil combined.

Using gas at home

Like all sources of heat and power gas must be treated with respect if accidents are to be prevented. These safety rules should be followed when using gas:

Buying an appliance Look to see if it carries one of these labels to guarantee safety and quality.

British Gas Seal of Approval

BSI Kitemark

Installation is an expert's job and should be carried out only by British Gas or a CORGI registered installer who guarantees his work to a high standard of safety and competence. The gas showroom has a list of CORGI fitters.

'Corgi' badge

Ventilation Gas appliances need to breathe in a supply of fresh air while they burn. This fresh air may be supplied by ventilators like these, which must never be blocked.

Door ventilator   Window ventilator   Air brick wall ventilator

Many gas appliances need a chimney or flue to carry away the fumes which are produced while the gas and fresh air are burning. This keeps the air in the room fresh for you to breathe. So if a gas fire is fitted in front of an existing chimney, the chimney must be swept first to remove any birds' nests, broken bricks, or soot.

Many new gas heaters, central heating boilers, and water heaters have a balanced flue which brings fresh air in from outside and carries fumes to the outside. These appliances must be fitted to an outside wall in the house. You may have seen flues outside houses with gas central heating.

Broken bricks, mortar, or soot can create danger by falling down the chimney and blocking it behind the fire.

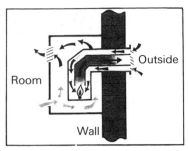

Balanced flue appliance

Servicing To keep gas appliances working safely and economically they need to be serviced, just like cars. Central heating boilers, fires, and water heaters should be checked once a year by British Gas or a CORGI installer.

Gas leaks If you smell gas at home and suspect a leak, this is what to do:

1 Put out cigarettes. Do not use matches or naked flames.
2 Do not operate electrical switches (including doorbells) either on or off.
3 Open doors and windows to get rid of the gas, and keep them open.
4 Check to see if a tap has been left on or a pilot light has blown out.
5 If not, there is probably a leak. Turn off the supply at the meter and call the gas service. (Under 'Gas' in the phone book.) Checking a suspected escape is free and simple gas escape repairs usually cost nothing.

If you smell gas in the street, report it at once. Do not leave it to someone else. The emergency service operates day and night.

Identity cards
All gas employees who need to call at customers' homes carry identity cards. Look at it carefully, to make sure that the caller is who he/she claims to be.

Help for disabled people
A special 'password' scheme is available for blind people so that they can check the true identity of the caller. The password is chosen by the customer and agreed with British Gas. Either British Gas or the local social welfare centre will give you details of how this scheme works.

A free safety check on gas appliances is available to anyone over 60 who lives alone, to a registered disabled person of any age who lives alone, or to anyone receiving a state disability benefit who lives alone. Many gas appliances can be fitted with special tap handles to make them easier to use. Braille and studded controls are also available.

Questions

1 **You want to change the position of the cooker in your kitchen. How do you find a competent gas service engineer to do this?**
2 **Why should a chimney be swept before a gas fire is fitted to an open fireplace?**
3 **What are the advantages of having a fire or heater with a balanced flue? Draw a diagram of how it works.**
4 **You come home one afternoon and there is a strong smell of gas in the house. Describe exactly what you would do.**
5 **Describe the facilities available to disabled people so that they can use gas safely and more easily.**

The gas meter

Gas is measured, at present, in cubic feet. The amount used in a house is measured on the gas meter, which often looks like this:

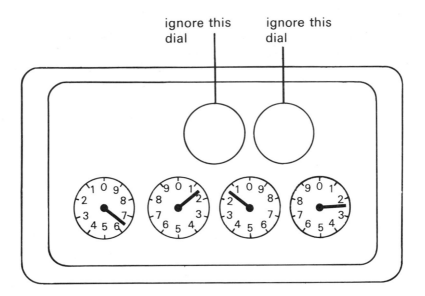

The reading on this meter is 6112.

How to read the gas meter

1 Ignore the two top dials.
2 Working from left to right, write down the smaller of the two figures between which the hand is pointing.
3 If the hand lies between 0 and 1 the smaller figure will be 0. If the hand lies between 9 and 0 the smaller figure will be 9.
4 When you have your 4-figure reading, add 00 after the reading. This is now your meter reading in cubic feet. The meter shown above therefore reads 611200.
5 Take away your last meter reading from this meter reading to find how many cubic feet of gas you have used since the last time your meter was read. Your gas bill will be based on the number of cubic feet you have used.

Newer meters
Some meters have a direct reading index which shows all the figures in a line, like this:

6	1	1	2	0	0

In some new houses, gas and electricity meters are outside the house in a locked cupboard, so that employees from the gas and electricity boards can read the meter even if you are out.

Measurement of gas is to be changed from cubic feet to cubic metres, but the method of reading the meter will be the same.

Payment

Gas meters are usually read once a quarter (every three months) and bills are sent out to customers after this. Budget schemes of different kinds are available to help you spread the cost of your bill. Page 140 describes some of these schemes.

The Gas Consumers' Council

This is an independent group which looks after the interests of all people who use gas. If you have any problems to do with gas, you should contact your local gas showroom or office. If you cannot sort your problem out, contact the Gas Consumers' Council whose address is on the back of your gas bill.

Questions

1 **What are the readings on the following gas meters?**

2 **How often are gas meters usually read and bills sent out to the consumer?**
3 **List the advantages of paying for your gas through a budget scheme.**

Electricity in the home

Using electricity safely

It would be hard to imagine life at home without electricity for lighting, heating, cooking, television and many other things.

But as well as being useful, electricity can also be dangerous. It can cause accidents and even death. All electrical appliances must be used properly and looked after carefully. You should make sure that everyone in your family follows these safety rules:

1 Never let water come into contact with electrical current. The combination of water and electricity is very dangerous. Do not let plugs or appliances become damp, or handle them with wet hands.
2 Avoid using adaptors if possible, and certainly do not overload them by plugging lots of appliances into them.
3 Only use good quality plugs that conform to British Standards.
4 Keep electrical equipment in good condition and do not use it if any of the wires or cords are frayed.
5 Do not attempt electrical repairs or wiring yourself. Your electricity board will have a list of expert electrical contractors in your area.
6 Make sure plugs are wired correctly and are fitted with the right size fuse (see below). Only wire plugs and mend fuses yourself if you know exactly what you are doing.
7 Look for the B.E.A.B. (British Electrotechnical Approvals Board) mark of safety on every electrical appliance you buy. Avoid buying second-hand appliances.

B.E.A.B. mark of safety

8 Special care is needed in the bathroom which can become damp and steamy.
   a Socket outlets are not allowed in bathrooms except special shaver sockets.
   b You must never carry any portable appliance (except a shaver) into the bathroom, even if it is plugged in outside. This includes hair-driers, electric fires, record players, heated rollers and so on. Ignoring this safety rule can cause fatal accidents.
   c The light should be operated by a pull-cord switch.
   d The radiant heaters made for bathrooms must be permanently fixed and wired to the wall, out of reach from the bath or shower, and operated by a pull-cord.

Plugs – fuses – earthing

How to wire a modern fused plug

Remember – The new colours are:

Green/Yellow to Earth
Brown   to Live
Blue   to Neutral

The old colours were:

Green to Earth
Red   to Live
Black to Neutral

Fuses

Electric current is carried around the house through wires specially laid for it. Fuses are just wires with a low melting point. They are there as a safety device. If a fault occurs and the current is too great for safety then the fuse will melt and break the circuit (the flow of electricity).

Modern appliances have a fuse within the plug. You should always fit a fuse of the correct size into the plug according to the wattage of the appliance.

Plug fuses are mainly either:

3 amp for most appliances up to 720 watts.

13 amp for most appliances between 720 and 3000 watts.

Earthing

Plugs and electrical wiring systems are fitted with an earth wire as a safety precaution.

Normally, the electric current travels along the path prepared for it, that is, along the wires. But if a fault occurs the electricity may leave this path and will instead take the shortest path to earth.

If the plug is fitted with an earth wire, then the current will run down to the earth through this earth wire, and not through the person holding the appliance.

Questions

1 **List five common causes of electrical accidents in the home.**
2 **How can you avoid electrical accidents in the home?**
3 **How would you get in touch with an electrical contractor who could safely rewire your house?**
4 **Why are fuses fitted into plugs and electrical wiring systems?**
5 **Explain how a fuse works.**
6 **What size fuse should you fit into the plug of:**
   a a 200 watt refrigerator
   b a lamp with a 100 watt bulb
   c a 1kW portable electric fire?
7 **Explain how an earth wire acts as a safety device.**
8 **Look inside the plug of an electrical appliance and see if it is correctly wired up as in the diagram above.**
   Check to see whether it has the correct size of fuse fitted.

The supply of electricity

Volts

Electricity is conducted, or flows, along wires from the generating station to the home. The pressure behind the flow is called the <u>voltage</u>. Supplies to houses in this country are about <u>240 volts</u>.

Units

The amount of electricity used in any house is measured by the meter. It is measured and paid for by the unit. If you had used 400 units of electricity and electricity cost 5p per unit, the cost to you would be 400 × 5p = £20.

Reading the meter

To find out how many units you have actually used in a quarter (three months) so that you can work out your bill, you read the meter. You then compare this reading with your last meter reading. The difference between the two gives you the number of units you have used. The reading on this meter is 72483.

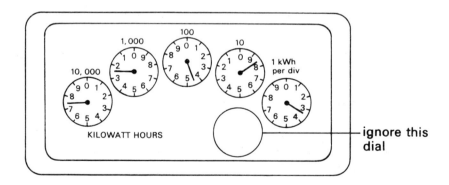

1   As with the gas meter (see page 30), when the hand lies between the two figures you read the smaller figure.
2   If the hand lies between 0 and 1 the smaller figure will be 0.
    If the hand lies between 9 and 0 the smaller figure will be 9.
3   The numbers on the dials are alternately clockwise and anti-clockwise.

Newer meters
Sometimes electric meters are simply read as a line of numbers, like some gas meters.

7	2	4	8	3

The cost of using electricity

Different electrical appliances need different amounts of power to make them work. For example, an electric cooker or fire needs more power than an electric light bulb.

Watts

The power of electricity is measured in watts. A cooker might need
12 000 watts to function, whereas a light bulb might need only 100 watts.
Electrical appliances have their wattage marked on them.

The amount of electricity any appliance uses (and so the amount it costs you
to run it) depends on two things:

1   The wattage (that is, the number of watts it uses).
2   The length of time you use it for.

Kilowatt

1000 watts are called a kilowatt (kW). One kW can be used for one hour for the
cost of one unit. Therefore: 1 unit = 1 kilowatt used for 1 hour.

A kilowatt hour means 1000 watts are used for 1 hour. If electricity costs 5p
per unit (that is, per kilowatt hour):

a 1000 watt (1 kW) fire will cost 5p to use for 1 hour.
a 500 watt iron will cost 2½p to use for 1 hour.
a 3 kW immersion heater will cost 15p to use for 1 hour.
a 250 watt food mixer will cost 1¼p to use for 1 hour.

Once you know the current cost of a unit, you can work out how much it will cost
you to use any electrical appliance.

Cheap electricity

If you use more electricity at night than during the day (e.g. with night storage
heaters, under-floor or ceiling heating systems, off-peak water heaters) it would
be sensible to have a special meter installed which provides you with much
cheaper electricity during the night, although the day-time rate is a little higher.
(See page 61.)

Easy payment schemes

These save you having to pay heavy quarterly bills by spreading the cost. The
schemes may include:

1   Regular, equal monthly payments.
2   Savings stamps bought from your electricity showroom.
3   Payments made of how much you like, when you like, at the showroom. The
    amount you pay is deducted from your bill before it is sent to you.

Questions

1   **Explain what these terms mean: (a) voltage, (b) unit.**
2   **How often are electricity bills usually paid?**
3   **Look at the information marked on any three electrical appliances, for
    example, cooker, food mixer and iron. At what voltage should each be
    used?**
4   **Your meter reading on 1 June was 84 671. Your meter reading on 1
    September is 85 391. If electricity costs 5p per unit, what will be the cost of
    the units used in this quarter?**
5   **Explain what these terms mean: (a) watts, (b) kilowatt, (c) kilowatt hour.**
6   **What two factors decide how much it will cost to use any electrical
    appliance?**
7   **Name four electrical appliances and for each state:**
    a the number of watts it uses.
    b how much it would cost to run for 1 hour at 5p per unit.

Conserving energy in your home

Whether you use gas, electricity, or any other fuel in your home the cost can be quite high. As well as this cost to ourselves we are using up the reserves of natural gas, coal, and oil which have taken many years to form, so it is wise to conserve energy as much as we can by using fuel carefully. Here are some suggestions to help you save energy and money.

Heating

Most of the money spent on fuel goes on heating. Pages 66–7 show ways of insulating your home so that you lose as little as possible of the heat you are paying for. You could reduce the cost of running your central heating by fitting room thermostats, a programmer or time clock (see page 59), radiator thermostats, and a hot water cylinder thermostat.

Other hints on heating that cost little or nothing are:

1   Only use heat when you need it. Turn heat down or off when you are out. Turn heating off in rooms you don't use and close the doors.
2   Don't block the radiators with furniture or long curtains.
3   Try turning down the thermostat a few degrees. But do not underheat where there are sick or elderly people, or babies.
4   Keep doors and windows closed, and draw curtains at night.
5   Fix aluminium foil behind radiators on outside walls to reflect heat back into the room. You can buy special foil, but kitchen foil will do.
6   If you do not have central heating, try to choose room heaters to suit the size of your rooms. Buy heaters fitted with a thermostat. Electric fires can be expensive to run, so check whether off-peak electric heaters or gas fires would suit you better.

Saving hot water

1   Lag the hot water tank (see page 67).
2   Keep the hot water thermostat at 60° C or less.
3   Turn the taps off properly and repair them if they drip. A fast dripping hot tap could waste enough water to fill a bath in a day.
4   Do not wash hands or dishes under running water. Use a bowl or put the plug in the sink or basin.
5   Have a shower instead of a bath, especially if your hot water comes from your central heating system rather than being separately heated by electricity.

Laundry

1   Wait until you have a full load of clothes before using your machine.
2   Some machines have a 'half-load' or 'economy' programme to save hot water and soap.
3   Special 'cool water' detergents wash well at much lower temperatures than normal. They save a lot of hot water.
4   Plan to do your ironing in one session. Start with a cooler setting and move on to hotter settings. Steam irons use a little more electricity.

Cooking

1 Careful planning means that more than one meal can be cooked at the same time and kept in the fridge or freezer. Try to fill the oven.
2 Gas ovens and fan-assisted electric ovens rarely need to be pre-heated for more than a couple of minutes. Do not open during cooking.
3 Use the right size of pan. It should just cover the ring of an electric cooker. If using gas, the flame should stay under the pan.
4 Once the contents have come to the boil, turn the heat down and keep the lid on. This keeps heat in and reduces condensation.
5 Cut vegetables up small so that they cook more quickly. Try cooking two vegetables in one pan, e.g. potatoes and carrots, carrots and peas.
6 A pressure cooker saves time and fuel.
7 Do not boil more water in a pan or kettle than you need. Be sure to cover the element in an electric kettle, but apart from this, boil just the right amount. Boiling a full kettle of water to make one cup of coffee wastes time and money.
8 Kettles should be descaled regularly, especially in hard water areas, otherwise you are wasting fuel by heating up the chalky deposits each time you boil it. Descalers are cheap to buy.
9 Some appliances cost much less to use than a full-sized oven, but you pay extra to buy them. Microwave ovens reheat and defrost food more cheaply than does an oven. An electric frying pan or a slow cooker can be cheaper to use than an oven and a toaster uses less fuel than a grill. It is cheaper to use the grill than the oven for small things like chops. An electric kettle is cheaper than a cooking ring for boiling water.

Fridges and freezers

1 Defrost regularly as a build-up of frost makes the appliance less efficient.
2 Do not set on a cooler setting than necessary.
3 Cool warm food before putting it inside.
4 Do not open doors unnecessarily or leave them open, letting the cold air out.
5 Load and unload a fridge or freezer as quickly as possible so that the cold air does not escape.
6 Do not run a fridge or freezer too large for your needs. Both should be kept at least ¾ full for greatest efficiency. If they are fairly empty the air circulates much more and the motor has to keep switching on to keep it cold. Fill up your freezer with bread if there is not much in it.

Lighting   See page 70.

Questions
1 **What are the two main reasons for using energy carefully in the home?**
2 **There are many ways of cutting heating costs. Choose and describe *three* that you would consider necessary if you were paying the heating bills.**
3 **Name three kinds of thermostat that can help control fuel costs.**
4 **You are looking for a new washing machine. What features would make it cheaper to run?**
5 **How can planning meals in advance help to save fuel costs?**
6 **Suggest five ways in which the hotplate of a cooker could be used more economically.**

The water supply

In the great majority of houses in this country you can have a constant supply of clean, pure water by simply turning on a tap.

Paying for the water

A lot of time and effort goes into providing this service, which is paid for by the water rates which every householder has to pay half-yearly. This rate may be paid separately or may be collected in with the general rates.

Other water services
The water authorities are also responsible for sewage disposal, for the prevention of water pollution, for fisheries and navigation, and for nature conservation and the provision of recreational facilities such as sailing and boating.

Collecting the water

Surface water
When rain falls on to hard ground it flows over the surface of the hillsides and forms small streams which flow together to form rivers and lakes.

Underground water
Some rain sinks down through porous ground until it reaches impermeable rock (which does not allow water to pass through it), then it collects to form large underground rivers and lakes.

Sources of pure water
Water authorities can collect water from any of these sources. Some sources of water are purer than others. Water is usually collected in large storage reservoirs on high land, or from deep underground lakes where it is likely to be clean and uncontaminated.

Contamination of water
As they flow farther downstream, rivers often become contaminated, especially near farmland and towns. Farm animals may pollute the water. Chemicals used on farm land, such as pesticides and fertilizers, drain through the soil and into streams and rivers. Factories may allow poisonous waste materials to flow into the rivers untreated.

    Obviously it is important to make sure that our drinking water is as pure as possible by collecting it from highland areas or underground lakes.

    Before the water is used, the water authorities treat it to make sure it is free from two main types of impurities.

1   It must be free from large objects, such as stones, fish or weed. These are removed by filtering the water through layers of gravel and sand.
2   The water must be free from bacteria which might cause diseases such as typhoid or dysentery. This is done by adding chlorine to the water in carefully measured amounts. Too little will not kill bacteria, too much will leave a taste, as in the swimming baths.

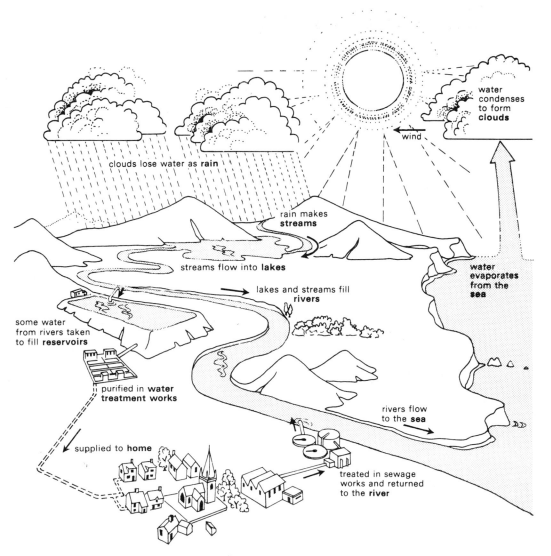

The water cycle

Some local authorities also add <u>fluoride</u> to the water to help prevent tooth decay in children. (See page 197.)

When the water has been fully treated it is piped to the town, often many miles away, in large underground pipes, and eventually it reaches your home.

Questions

1 **Who pays for the provision of a pure water supply, and how often?**
2 **List some of the other services provided by the water authority.**
3 **How are underground rivers and lakes formed?**
4 **Name two sources of water which are likely to be fairly pure.**
5 **Why does river water become more contaminated as it flows downstream?**
6 **Why is water filtered through sand and gravel beds?**
7 **Why are (a) chlorine, and (b) fluoride added to the water supply?**

Hard and soft water

What is hard water?

You will know if you live in, or visit, an area supplied with hard water because when you try to wash your hands with soap you will find it difficult to get the soap to make a good lather. You will find scum forming around the wash basin or bath. A hard, chalky deposit called 'fur' will form inside the kettle, and this will make the kettle feel heavy even when it is empty.

Why does this happen?
The water is like this basically because it contains mineral salts dissolved in it. When rainwater falls on to certain soils such as limestone or chalk, it sinks through the soil dissolving some of the limestone or chalk as it passes through. When this water is collected from underground and piped to your home, it still contains these dissolved salts.

The disadvantages of hard water

1 As it is difficult to produce a lather with hard water, you have to use more soap and more detergents, so it costs you more money.
2 Hard water is much more harsh on your skin and hair. Washing your hair and skin in soft water makes them feel soft and silky.
3 Clothes washed in soft water feel softer to touch, and it is easier to rinse soap powders or detergents away. Most washing powders and liquids now have water softeners added to them, to make washing easier for people in hard water areas.
4 Hard water causes the inside of the kettle to 'fur up'. When you put the kettle on to heat water you have to heat the chalky layer as well as the water, so it will take longer and use more fuel. You can buy preparations from a hardware shop which will remove the fur quite easily.

5 The boiler and pipes can fur up, sometimes causing a complete blockage. This is more difficult and more expensive to remove than the fur in a kettle.
6 Scum will form around the edge of the bath or wash basins when you try to wash with soap. It is unpleasant in appearance and makes the bath more difficult to clean.

The two types of hard water

The mineral salts causing hard water are mainly calcium bicarbonate, magnesium bicarbonate, calcium sulphate and magnesium sulphate.

Temporary hard water
This contains calcium and magnesium bicarbonates. This water can be softened by boiling. When the water is heated calcium bicarbonate changes to calcium carbonate (chalk) and magnesium bicarbonate changes to magnesium carbonate. As these are not soluble in water they fall as a deposit. This is not serious in the kettle and can quite easily be removed, but hot water boilers and pipes can become so furred up that they get completely blocked.

If you live in an area where the water is very hard you will need to have the deposit cleared from the pipes and boiler every few years.

Permanent hard water
This contains calcium and magnesium sulphates. It cannot be softened by boiling but it can be softened by adding washing soda (sodium carbonate), borax or bath salts to your washing water. These change the dissolved salts into a fine powder, so that the water itself is left soft.

A water softening system

If you live in an area where the water is very hard and causes you a lot of inconvenience, it may be worth installing a rather expensive water softening system, which works using a resin such as permutite.

This system softens *all* the water as it enters the house, so it prevents the furring of pipes as well as providing soft water for washing. It works in the following way. All the water coming into the house passes through a container full of the resin, and is softened by it before passing through the pipes in the house. After a while the resin becomes exhausted and has to be recharged with a solution of ordinary salt.

Questions
1 **List all the points by which householders would realize they were living in a hard water area.**
2 **Outline in your own words how hard water is caused.**
3 **Imagine you live in an area where the water is very hard. Describe what you consider are the three main disadvantages of your water supply.**
4 **How do detergent manufacturers help people in hard water areas when they make their products?**
5 **What are the mineral salts which cause temporary hard water?**
6 **How can temporary hard water be softened?**
7 **When a kettle of temporary hard water is boiled, what happens to the salts dissolved in the water?**
8 **What are the mineral salts which cause permanent hard water?**
9 **Name three products which will soften this water.**
10 **Describe *how* these products soften the water.**
11 **What is the advantage of having water softening equipment installed in your house rather than just softening the water as you use it?**
12 **Explain how this type of water softening system works.**

The removal of liquid waste

Household waste can be divided into two types, liquid waste and dry waste. The local authority is responsible for disposing of this waste. They pay for this with money from the rates.

Years ago, before there was organized refuse collection and main drains and sewers, people in towns and cities often had no way of disposing of their refuse except by throwing it into the streets. This made the streets smell unpleasant, and encouraged the spread of rats, flies and other pests and disease-carrying bacteria.

The disposal of liquid waste: drainage

Three types of liquid waste have to be disposed of from the home:

1 Waste from the lavatory.
2 Household water from the sink, bath and wash basin.
3 Storm water (rain water which falls on the roof).

Waste from the lavatory

When the W.C. is flushed, the water forces away the contents, leaving clean water in the S-bend at the bottom of the pan. This water prevents smells and insects from the drains coming back up the pipes into the house.

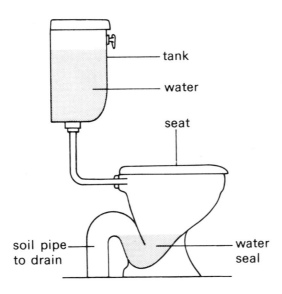

The pipe from the W.C. is a wide pipe to allow for the efficient flushing away of all waste matter. It leads into a vertical soil pipe. The top of the soil pipe is open for ventilation and must extend above the level of the roof. It leads down below the ground, enclosed all the time, and then to the main drains which run under the street.

Between the house and the main sewer under the street, there is an inspection chamber covered with an iron manhole cover. This allows access to the drains if it is necessary.

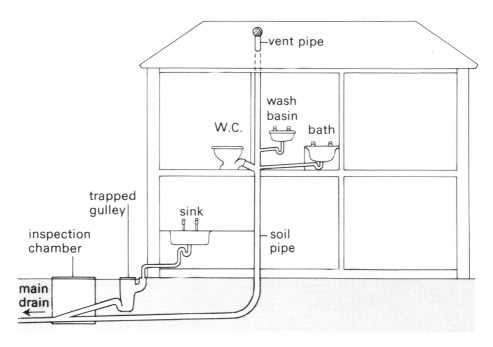

The household water drainage system

Water from sink, bath and wash basin

This water can be drained away in narrower pipes than those from the W.C. Below all sinks and wash basins there is a U-bend in the pipe which is always full of water. This stops smells coming up from the drains and is useful if pipes become blocked. There is a plug or 'cleaning eye' at the base which can be undone to empty the trap, so that any blockage can be easily removed.

In modern houses, the water from the wash basin and bath joins the soil pipe and leads to the main sewer. Waste water from the kitchen sink runs straight down a pipe into an open drain outside.

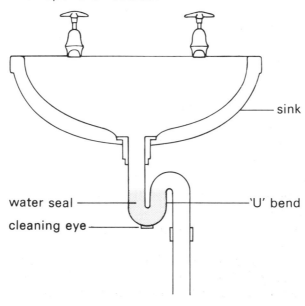

Storm water

In order to help keep the home dry, the rain falling on to the roof of the house is collected in gutters and runs down pipes on the outside wall of the house into an open drain. This either then goes to the main sewer under the street, or, as it is quite clean and harmless, it is sometimes just drained away into the soil.

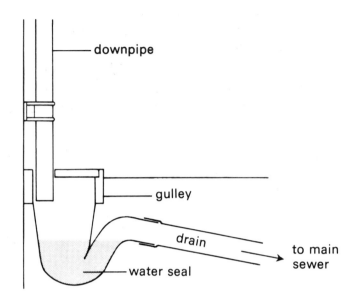

Keeping the drainage system clean and hygienic

As all parts of the drainage system are concerned with removing waste matter which may contain millions of bacteria it is obviously important to keep them as clean and fresh-smelling as possible.

The W.C.

The W.C. must be kept clean and hygienic to prevent the spread of the bacteria present in human excreta which cause sickness and disease.

1 The lavatory pan can be keptclean with a specially shaped brush kept only for this purpose.
2 Special powder or liquid cleaners containing bleach can be used in the pan.
3 The lavatory seat and the handles of the cistern and door must be regularly disinfected as bacteria are likely to be transferred on to them from people's hands.
4 Hands must be washed after every visit to the lavatory. Children should be trained to do this.

The sink

The sink must be carefully cleaned after use to keep it free from particles of food and grease.

1 After washing up, the sink and draining board should be washed down with hot soapy water.
2 Clean water should be run through the sink to make sure that the water in the U-bend is fresh and clean.
3 A few drops of disinfectant can be put down the sink daily to kill bacteria.

Blocked sinks

Sometimes a sink becomes blocked and the water runs away very slowly, or not at all. If this happens you can take the following action:

1   Remove any pieces of food which may be blocking the sink outlet.
2   Use a plunger vigorously over the outlet, and try to dislodge the blockage.

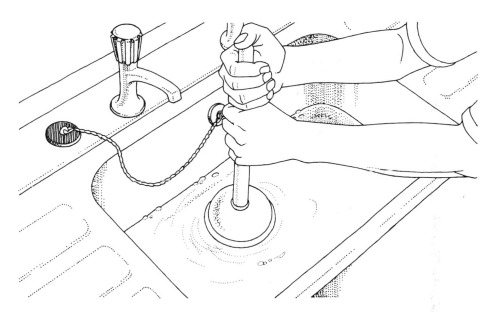

3   If this does not work, you can unscrew the plug under the U-bend below the sink and you may find the cause of the blockage. Remember that the water in the U-bend will come out when you do this, so be sure to have a bucket ready to catch it.
4   Caustic soda crystals can be put down the drain. This will clear most blockages, but it must be used with extreme caution as it can cause severe burns to the skin.
5   If all these measures fail, you will have to call a plumber, or a commercial firm specializing in unblocking pipes and drains.

Outside drains

Remove litter and leaves from the drain regularly. Pour a hot solution of soda water or disinfectant down once a week, to prevent smells.

Questions

1   **What are the three types of liquid waste which have to be removed from the home?**
2   **Describe how waste is removed from the W.C., illustrating your answer with a diagram.**
3   **Draw a diagram to show the U-bend below a sink or wash basin. Explain why it is there.**
4   **How and why should the W.C. be cleaned daily?**
5   **When washing up after a meal, how should you clean the sink?**
6   **How can you prevent your sink becoming blocked? What could you do to clear a blockage?**

Sewage disposal

Once the liquid waste leaves the drains of each house it passes into the sewers under the street leading to the sewage works.

When it gets there it has to be treated to make it harmless. The harmful bacteria in the sewage have to be destroyed and this is done slowly by the natural action of other bacteria and air on the sewage.

The sewage flows into tanks where bacteria begin to break it down. The sludge, or more solid matter, gradually sinks to the bottom of the tank and separates from the liquid.

The sludge is removed and further treated by bacteria to make it harmless. It is dried and rotted and can be sold as fertilizer provided it does not contain harmful chemical waste from factories.

The liquid is acted upon further by bacteria in the air, until it becomes harmless. Then it is allowed to flow into rivers.

Sewage works

Chemical pollution

Although these processes make the sewage free from harmful bacteria, they cannot always treat chemical substances which may have entered the waste. The Water Authorities make a constant effort to keep our rivers and seas free from pollution.

You can sometimes see froth floating on rivers; this may come from detergents which could not be broken down by the processes in the sewage works. Manufacturers of washing powders now produce detergents which are 'biodegradable' and can be broken down and made harmless by natural biological action. All British detergents for domestic use are biodegradable, although detergents used in industry may still cause pollution.

Septic tanks and cesspits

Some houses in country areas are not connected to the main drains and sewers. Their waste is normally drained to a septic tank or a cesspit.

Septic tanks

Septic tanks normally consist of two pits below ground level. The sewage drains from the house into the first tank where bacterial action slowly breaks the sewage down to a more liquid form. The heavier part of the liquid, or sludge, gradually sinks to the bottom of the tank and is later removed by the local authority. The liquid part passes into the second pit where further bacterial action slowly makes it harmless. After this has happened, the clean effluent is drained away into the ground.

Cesspits

A cesspit is a pit below the ground, situated well away from the house. It must be watertight, ventilated and have a removable cover for emptying. All the sewage from the house is drained into the pit which is emptied when necessary by the local authority. A suction hose drains the sewage into a covered cart similar to the type used for cleaning street drains. It is then taken to the nearest sewage works for treatment.

Questions

1 **Explain briefly how sewage is treated to make it harmless.**
2 **How are the solid and liquid parts of sewage disposed of after they have been treated?**
3 **What is a 'biodegradable' detergent?**
4 **Describe two ways of disposing of sewage hygienically in households which are not connected to main drains.**

The removal of household refuse

Dustbins

The contents of a householder's dustbin may include a variety of materials, including broken glass and china, food, peelings, paper, plastic and ashes. Garden rubbish should not be put into the bin. It should either be burned or rotted down in a compost heap and then used to enrich the soil.

Dustbins may be made of various materials:
1   *Galvanized metal bins.* These are hardwearing but noisy. The lids may be metal, but are sometimes made of plastic or rubber, which are much quieter in use and do not dent if dropped.
2   *Plastic bins.* These are lighter and less noisy, but you cannot put hot ashes into them and they can blow over if it is very windy.
3   *Plastic or paper sacks*, in wire mesh containers, are used in some areas. The whole bag is removed and replaced by a new one once a week. This method is clean, but the bags are easy to damage.

Care of the bin

It is important to keep the dustbin as clean and hygienic as you can, because otherwise it makes an ideal place for bacteria and flies to breed.

You should follow all these rules:
1   Make sure the lid fits firmly, to keep out flies, vermin (rats and mice), dogs and cats, and to keep the contents dry.
2   Wrap all damp waste such as vegetable peelings in paper before putting them into the bin, or they will stick to its sides.
3   Wash tins before putting them into the bin. Do not put other rubbish inside them, as tins are often removed by magnets later and sold as scrap metal.
4   Stand the dustbin on bricks to help ventilate it.
5   Scrub the bin out regularly with disinfectant. Allow it to dry before re-using it.
6   Line the bottom of the bin with thick layers of newspaper before putting refuse in, to help keep it clean.

Paper salvage

If you have a lot of clean paper and card, put it out separately from the rest of your rubbish, as many local authorities can sell clean paper for recycling.

Rubbish chutes

Large blocks of flats normally have a central rubbish chute with an opening in or near each kitchen. The refuse goes down the chute into very large bins which are emptied into dustcarts fitted with mechanical lifting devices.

Waste disposal units

Some sinks have a waste disposal unit fitted underneath them. Most waste, including bones and broken china but excluding cans, string and cloth, can be put into them. Electrically driven knives grind it to a fine pulp and it is washed away down the sink. It is a simple and hygienic way of disposing of refuse, but can be expensive to buy and install.

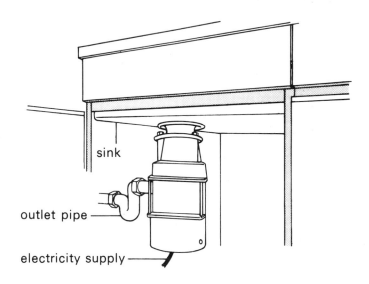

Safety

It is important to choose a waste disposal unit which will be safe in use. The safest kind will only work when the guard lid is in position. This avoids the possibility of children putting not only rubbish but also their hands on to the sharp blades. The electrical on/off switch should always be positioned out of reach of children.

Questions

1 **What are the advantages and disadvantages of the different types of dustbins you can use?**
2 **How would you keep a plastic dustbin clean?**
3 **Describe how a waste disposal unit works.**

Refuse disposal

The disposal of the contents of the householders' bins is organized by the local authority and is paid for from the rates. They may dispose of the waste in various ways:

Dumping at sea

Towns near the coast may dump rubbish in the sea, far enough out to prevent it being washed back on to the beaches.

Rubbish tips or dumps

In some areas, all the rubbish is tipped into large pits in the ground. It may be burned, and then covered with a layer of earth, until the pit is filled. When one is full another pit is used.

Although this method of disposal is simple and cheap, it is not very satisfactory. The rubbish may be blown around by the wind, and it can smell unpleasant and attract rats and flies looking for food. It is, however, a method quite widely used in country areas where there is more space to situate the tip away from houses.

Rubbish tip

Refuse disposal plants

The most modern plants will sort mechanically from the refuse any materials which can be sold.

The money obtained from selling the refuse helps to keep the cost of operating the service as low as possible, and so this both prevents waste and saves money for the ratepayer.

Modern refuse disposal plant

Materials which can be salvaged

These vary, according to the mechanical equipment installed at the plant. A modern 'reclamation plant' could salvage some of the following:

1 Some metals, for example tin cans, can be removed by magnets.
2 Paper and plastics can be formed into pellets and sold as industrial fuel.
3 Items which cannot be burned, such as pieces of concrete or broken china, can be used for filling in land which is being prepared for building sites, or after quarrying.
4 Ashes produced after burning waste can be used by farmers on the land.
5 Some refuse disposal plants can use the heat from their incinerators to provide their own heating.
6 In some plants the heat may be used to work electric generators, but this is not often economical.

Questions

1 **List some of the ways in which local authorities dispose of the rubbish from dustbins. What are (a) the advantages, and (b) the disadvantages of each method?**
2 **Who pays for the disposal of refuse?**
3 **Name four of the materials which can be salvaged from household rubbish for sale or re-use.**

Further work on chapter 2

1   Have a look at some of the electrical appliances in your home to find out the wattage of each. Make a list in order, from lowest to highest. Can you draw any conclusions about running costs from this?

2   Your parents are tired of paying ever-increasing fuel bills and have decided to spend some money on insulating your home to keep in the heat. Look around your home and see what you can suggest.

3   Look at a recent gas or electricity bill for your home and see if you can work out how the final total is reached. If you were responsible for paying the bill yourself, suggest what steps you could take to keep costs down.

4   Look around your home and see if you can trace the route of the drainage pipes that carry waste water away from the kitchen sink, washbasin, toilet, and the rain water from the roof.

5   Make a study of any subject related to this chapter, for example, the fluoridation of water; conservation; pollution; the arguments for coal- or nuclear-powered electricity generating stations; alternative energy sources; getting oil and gas from under the sea.

Sources of further information

You can send to the following for a list of the material they publish, often free of charge. (Enclose a stamped addressed envelope.) It may include booklets, videos, workcards, films, computer software, and so on:

British Gas Education Service, PO Box 46, Hounslow, Middlesex TW4 6NF.

The Electricity Council, 30 Millbank, London SW1P 4RD.

Department of Energy, Energy Efficiency Office, Room 312, Thames House South, Millbank, London SW1P 4QJ.

Friends of the Earth, 377 City Road, London EC1V 1NA. There are many local groups you can join. Interests include wildlife, energy, and mineral conservation.

Films for hire or sale
EFVA National Audio Visual Aids Library, George Building, Normal College, Bangor LL57 2PZ. Films available on fuel, energy (including solar energy), and alternatives.

Concord Films Council Ltd., 201 Felixstowe Road, Ipswich, Suffolk. Films available on energy, conservation, solar energy in the home, etc.

Focal Point Visual Ltd., 251 Copnor Road, Hants PO3 5EE. Films on pollution and conservation.

Computer software
Cambridge Micro Software, Edinburgh Building, Shaftesbury Road, Cambridge CB2 2RU. Includes 'Watts in your Home'.

Chapter 3

Heating the home

Fires and heaters

Heat transferred from any fire or heater reaches the people in the room either by <u>radiation</u> or <u>convection</u>.

Radiated heat

This warms only the solid objects or people it shines on. It does not warm the air between them, nor does it warm the backs of the people or objects it shines on. The sun warms the earth by radiant heat, and a bar electric fire warms by radiant heat.

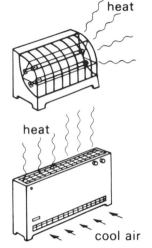

Convected heat

This works on the principle of warm air currents rising from the heater and being replaced by cooler air. Currents of air circulate around the room, gradually warming both the air and the people in the room.

We can keep ourselves and our homes warm either by individual fires and heaters, or by central heating. We shall look at central heating systems later in the chapter; we shall now look at the many types of fires and heaters that are available, using solid fuel, gas, electricity or oil.

Solid-fuel fires

Open coal fires
Advantages

1 A coal fire has a cheerful, attractive appearance.
2 It can have a back boiler to supply hot water.
3 It helps to ventilate the room. A coal fire needs air to burn, so it is constantly drawing air into the room to replace the air it uses.

Disadvantages

1 A lot of heat goes up the chimney and is wasted.
2 A coal fire causes dust, ashes and soot in the home.
3 A lot of work is involved in cleaning and laying the fire, in stoking it, and in having the chimney swept.
4 As it warms by radiation, only people directly facing the fire will be warm. Their backs may feel cold and people away from the fire may feel cold.
5 It causes a draught in the room as it draws in the air it needs to burn.
6 When the fire is not lit there will be no hot water unless an electric immersion heater is fitted in the hot water tank.
7 Smoke from coal fires causes pollution of the air. This is a health hazard and also causes damage to the stonework of buildings.

Enclosed solid-fuel fires or room heaters
The glow of the fire shows through glass doors. These
fires use Solid Smokeless Fuel. This fuel is made from
coal which has been treated so that it does not
produce smoke.

Advantages
1   These fires are quite economical to run as they can be easily controlled.
2   They do not waste as much heat up the chimney as an open fire does.
3   They can heat the hot water and several radiators.
4   The surface of the heater gets hot and sets up convection currents which warm
    the whole room.

Disadvantages
1   The fires are not very attractive to look at.
2   The fire has to be stoked and the ashes cleaned out.
3   The fuel has to be ordered, stored and carried in.

Smokeless zones

Many areas are now smoke controlled, which means that no houses or
factories in the area may burn coal or any fuel which produces smoke. This was
enforced by the Clean Air Act of 1956 to try to eliminate the problem of smog.
Smog was produced by the mixture of heavy fog with smoke from hundreds of
chimneys which could not escape up into the air through the fog. This smog
was extremely unhealthy and caused the deaths of many people from
bronchitis and other diseases of the lungs.

Gas fires

Modern gas fires use both radiant and convected heat to warm the room. They
have to be fitted into either an existing fireplace with a chimney, or an external
wall with a flue to ensure adequate ventilation.

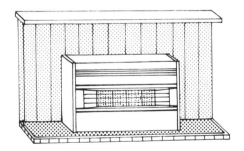

Advantages
1   They are simple to use and control, and usually light automatically.
2   They warm the room quickly.
3   Some can heat the hot water if fitted in a fireplace where there is an existing
    back boiler.
4   Some models can run a central heating system.
5   Their appearance is attractive.

Disadvantages

1 About 25% of the heat produced is lost up the chimney or flue.
2 They should be serviced every two or three years.

Mobile gas heaters

These run from bottled gas, e.g. Calor gas. They are not very attractive to look at, but they give off a lot of heat. They are on castors, so they can be moved to wherever you want them. Anyone living temporarily in a house without a good heating system would find them ideal, as when you move house you can take them with you. The bottles of gas are bought in advance, so you avoid unexpectedly high fuel bills.

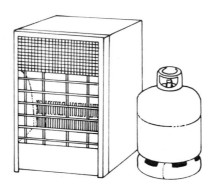

Electric fires

There are many different kinds of electric fires and heaters available, including fan heaters, radiant fires, convector heaters, and oil-filled portable radiators which are electrically heated. (Night storage heaters also use electricity. These are discussed in the section on central heating. See page 60.)

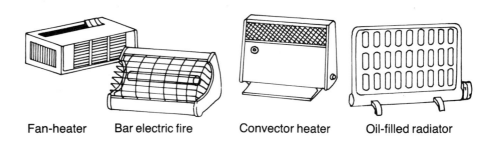

| Fan-heater | Bar electric fire | Convector heater | Oil-filled radiator |

Advantages

1 Electric fires are very clean and easy to use.
2 They are very efficient, as no heat is wasted up the chimney.
3 Most heaters can be carried to where they are required.
4 They are useful for heating a small area quickly.

Disadvantages

1 They are expensive to run for a long time or for a large area.
2 They do not heat the water

Oil heaters

These may be either the convector type, similar to electric convector heaters, or the radiant type. The fuel they use is paraffin.

Convector oil heater

Radiant oil heater

Advantages

1 They are the cheapest form of heating to buy and to run.
2 You can carry the heaters to wherever you need the heat.
3 Fuel must be bought before it is used, so you avoid unexpected bills.

Disadvantages

1 They are not very attractive to look at.
2 Some heaters give off an unpleasant smell.
3 They need to be refilled fairly often.
4 They produce a lot of moisture as they burn, and so can encourage dampness and condensation.
5 They can be very dangerous and cause many fires; sometimes the heater is knocked over when alight, or a draught blowing on the heater causes the flame to set fire to material such as curtains.

The Consumer Protection Act 1961 was passed in an attempt to prevent such fires. It lays down safety standards for all gas, electric and oil heaters now sold. When you go to buy an oil heater you should only buy one marked with the British Standards Institution Kitemark. It will only have this mark if it is safe and:

a has a reliable guard.
b cannot be knocked over easily.
c the flame will go out immediately if it should be knocked over.

Questions

1 **What four fuels are used for heating?**
2 **What is meant by radiant heat?**
3 **Describe, with a diagram, how convected heat warms the whole room.**
4 **Why do some people like a coal fire better than any other kind of heating, yet others dislike coal fires?**
5 **What are the advantages of an enclosed solid-fuel fire as compared with an open coal fire?**
6 **Why was the Clean Air Act of 1956 passed?**
7 **What are the points for and against heating a room with a gas fire?**
8 **What kind of gas heater would suit a couple living temporarily in a flat without a good heating system?**
9 **Describe and draw two electric heaters. Say where each would be useful.**
10 **Why should you choose an oil heater with the B.S.I. Kitemark?**

Central heating

Central heating is a system where heat from just one central source is carried around the whole house.

The systems most commonly used are:
a A series of radiators around the house containing hot water. The water may be heated by solid fuel, gas or oil.
b A system which blows warm air into the rooms.
c Night storage heaters and under-floor heating using off-peak electricity. Night storage heaters are not exactly central heating, but we can look at them here.

New houses

Nearly all new houses have a central heating system built into them. When choosing a new house you should try to find out whether the system installed will suit your needs.

Installing heating

If you decide to install central heating in an existing house it will be expensive, but it adds to the comfort and value of the house. Before you decide on the type to install you should get as much information as you can to compare the different kinds on the market. There is always plenty of advice available from gas and electricity board showrooms and from suppliers of solid fuel and oil.

You should carefully consider all the following general points before making your final decision:

1 How much will the system cost to buy and install?
2 What will the approximate running costs be each week?
3 How often should it be serviced?
4 Is it easy to work?
5 Will it cause much dirt in the house?
6 Does the system provide hot water or will a separate water heating system be required?
7 Is it easy to control the heat for economical running?
8 Will it produce enough heat for the whole house, even in the coldest weather?

Small bore central heating system

This is a system of radiators filled with hot water. The water may be heated by various means:
a gas, oil or solid-fuel boiler
a gas or solid-fuel fire.

The water is forced through the small pipes to the radiators by means of a small electric pump.

All of these systems provide domestic hot water (for baths, washing and laundry) by the indirect system. This water never mixes with the water in the radiators (see page 63).

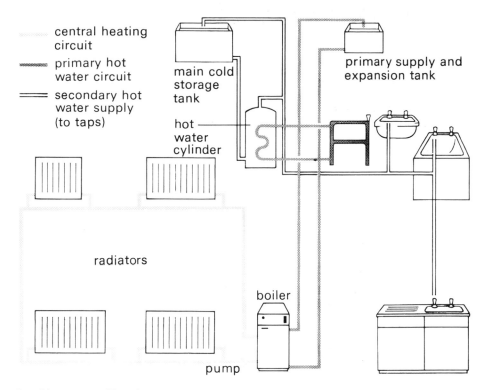

central heating circuit

primary hot water circuit

secondary hot water supply (to taps)

main cold storage tank

hot water cylinder

radiators

boiler

pump

primary supply and expansion tank

Small bore central heating system

Thermostats

Most systems can be fitted with thermostatic control. The thermostat is fixed to the wall of the room and set to the required temperature, for example, 20°C. When the room reaches this temperature the pump switches off. When the temperature falls below 20°C it switches back on. This helps keep running costs down.

Time clocks

These are often used with central heating systems. They enable the heating to switch itself on and off automatically at the time you set the clock. This means, for example, that if you came home from work at 6 p.m. you could set the clock to switch on at 4.30 p.m. so that the house would be warm for your return.

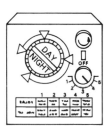

The warm air system

The air is warmed in a gas heating unit and then blown by an electric fan through metal ducts around the house. The hot air enters each room through grilles in the wall or floor.

As the warm air is carried around the house in large metal ducts, it is not suitable for existing houses but is fitted while a house is being built.

This system can also be fitted with a thermostat and time clock.

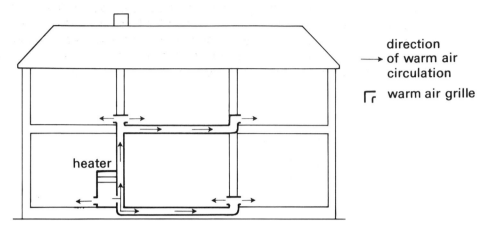

$\longrightarrow$ direction of warm air circulation

⌐ᵣ warm air grille

Central heating systems run by electricity

Night storage heaters

These heaters are filled with firebricks with an electric element running through them. The electric current heats up the bricks during the night when electricity is cheaper, and slowly gives out the heat during the next day. A separate heater is installed in every room where one is required.

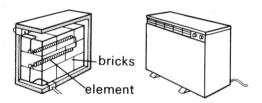

bricks

element

Advantages

1   They are fairly cheap to buy and install.
2   As they use 'off-peak' electricity, which costs less than electricity used during the day, they are not too expensive to run.
3   It is now possible to control the power input.
4   If you are out of the house all day, the modern type can be set to give out a small amount of heat during the day and more in the evening.
5   They are clean, easy and quiet to use.

Disadvantages

1   They used to be large and extremely heavy. Modern ones are smaller.
2   The heat cannot be quickly controlled.
3   The old-fashioned type give off all the heat during the day.
4   They do not supply hot water.

Under-floor heating, overhead ceiling heating
An electric element is embedded either into the concrete floor or into the ceiling panels when the house is being built. This system also normally uses off-peak electricity.

Economy 7

The Economy 7 tariff has two unit prices – one for day, one for night. The night-time (or 'off-peak') rate costs less than half the standard domestic rate. The day-time rate costs slightly more than the standard rate. It is wise to have an Economy 7 meter fitted if a home is heated by storage heaters or if the water heating system can take advantage of the seven hours of off-peak electricity. This system is most useful for the family who are at home all day.

Questions

1   **What is the difference between central heating and a fire?**
2   **What are the advantages of central heating?**
3   **Describe the six most important points to consider when installing central heating.**
4   **You have decided to install a small bore central heating system in your house. What method would you choose for heating the water which circulates in the system? List all the advantages of the method you have chosen.**
5   **Describe how a thermostat works and the advantages of having one.**
6   **Why are time-clocks often fitted to heating systems? Give an example of when one would be useful.**
7   **Name three central heating systems which have to be installed while the house is being built.**
8   **You are living in a house built several years ago which at present is heated by open coal fires. Describe one type of central heating which you could install, giving the reasons why the system is suitable.**
9   **An elderly retired couple wish to install a central heating system. What kind would you advise them to choose and what would be its advantages for them?**
10 **Name a central heating system which supplies hot water for domestic use while it warms the house.**
11 **What is 'off-peak' electricity?**
12 **What are the advantages of the Economy 7 tariff?**

The domestic hot water supply

A constant supply of hot water is a great advantage to any household. There are many different methods of heating the water, using solid fuel, gas, electricity or oil. Some methods are combined with the heating of the house, while others work independently of it.

   When you move into a house there is usually a hot water system installed. If not, you should make careful enquiries to find the system best suited to your particular needs. You should consider these points:

1   The cost of buying the equipment and having it installed.
2   The probable running costs.
3   Suitability for the size and type of family, e.g. how much hot water is required? how often is the family in or out all day?
4   Is the system easy to use?
5   How long does the water take to heat?

The direct hot water system

In older houses hot water may be provided by a solid-fuel boiler in the kitchen or an open coal fire in the living-room. The water is heated in a small back boiler behind the fire. It rises to and is stored in the cylinder. From there it goes directly to the hot taps.

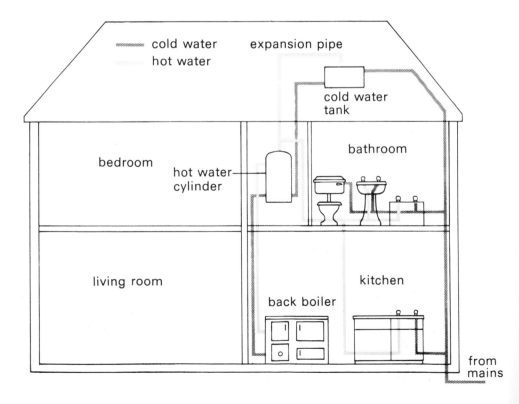

cold water
hot water
expansion pipe
cold water tank
bedroom
hot water cylinder
bathroom
living room
back boiler
kitchen
from mains

The indirect hot water system

All central heating systems which provide hot water use the indirect method of water heating. Look again at the central heating diagram on page 59.

In this system, the boiler heats water which flows through a coiled pipe inside the hot water tank and back to the boiler. The water in the cylinder is heated by contact with these coiled hot pipes, and is then used to supply the taps. The water in the coiled pipe never changes but passes continually around the system. Being in a closed ciruit it never mixes with the hot water supply to the taps.

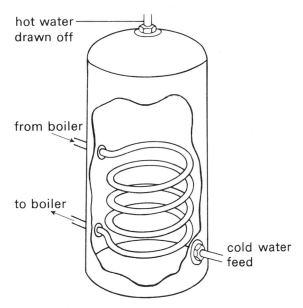

Hot water cylinder heated by coiled pipe

The advantages of the indirect system are:

1 It makes sure that the water inside the radiators, which may become rather rusty, never comes through the taps for household use.
2 It prevents the constant 'furring' of the pipes and boiler, as the same (specially softened water) passes continually through the boiler. This is particularly important in hard water areas where the whole system might otherwise fur up.

Hot water only
If hot water only is required, and not the central heating, the pump which circulates the water around the radiators can just be switched off.

Heating water by electricity

This has several advantages:

1 It is very efficient and wastes little heat, as the element is completely immersed in the water. All the heat goes into the water and none is wasted through flues or chimneys.
2 It is clean, easy to use, and easy to control.

But it can be expensive to use electricity to supply constant, large quantities of hot water.

Different types of electric water heater

1 *Immersion heaters* have an element fitted into the tank like an electric kettle. A twin-immersion heater is very economical to use. This type has two elements, one short and one long. The shorter one heats the top of the tank only and provides plenty of water for daily use. The longer element need only be switched on when large quantities are required for baths and doing the washing.

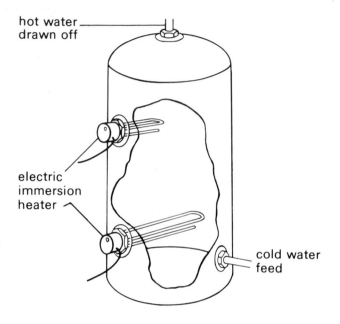

hot water drawn off

electric immersion heater

cold water feed

2 *Storage water heaters* can be fitted near the sink or wash basin, providing smaller or larger quantities of hot water according to their size. These are useful in older houses which do not have a hot water system.

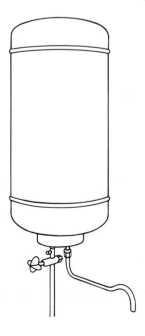

Heating water by gas

Gas water heaters are mainly of the <u>instantaneous</u> type. They supply endless hot water to one or several taps. When the tap is turned on the cold water passes through a series of narrow pipes which are heated by gas jets. There is no hot water cylinder for storing water with this system as the water is heated instantly and only when required.

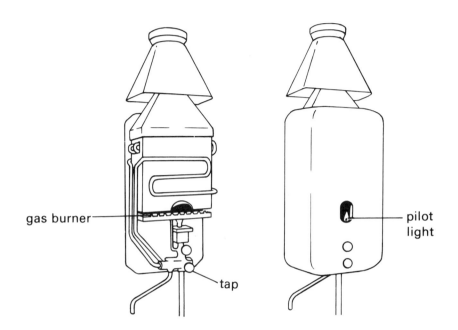

gas burner

tap

pilot light

Gas fires may have a boiler fitted behind them, so that they heat the water as well as the room. These are often installed when a coal fire with a back boiler is being replaced by a gas fire.

Gas storage water heaters are also available. The water is heated by a circulator and stored in the hot water cylinder until required. Some gas central heating systems also provide hot water (see page 58).

Questions

1 **How do central heating systems provide hot water?**
2 **What are the points for and against heating water by electricity?**
3 **Why is a twin-immersion heater quite an economical method of water heating for a family?**
4 **You have moved to a flat which has cold water only. What kind of water heater could be installed to give a plentiful supply of hot water to the kitchen sink?**
5 **Describe, with the help of a diagram, how an instantaneous gas water heater works.**

Insulation

Fuel bills can be very high however you heat your home, so you do not want to waste heat. Good insulation will cut down the amount of heat loss from the house.

Heat loss can be prevented in the following ways:

1 **Insulate your loft**

Heat from the house will rise upwards and escape through the roof. A layer of glass fibre or 'loose-fill' insulating material, 75 mm (3") thick will prevent some of this loss. The insulation is easy to lay and the cost of it should be recovered by money saved on fuel after two or three years. Do not insulate <u>below</u> the cold water tank if it is in the loft, as some warmth from the house is needed to prevent the water tank from freezing in winter.

2 **Draughts**

Draughts waste heat and make you feel uncomfortable. They can be prevented by fitting plastic, foam or metal excluder strips around doors and windows.

3 **Cavity walls**

These can be filled with special insulating material to cut down heat loss through the walls. You must choose an approved contractor (covered by an Agrément Certificate) to do the work for you. The contractor will make sure that the walls are suitable for treatment and will guarantee a good job. The work takes about a day and is carried out from the outside by drilling the outer wall, so no mess is caused inside the house.

4 Double glazing

This consists of two panes of glass with a sealed air space between them. It cuts down heat loss through windows and reduces noise and condensation. It makes the room feel more comfortable as the area near the window does not feel cold.

Double glazing is very expensive, and it would take many years to recover the cost in money saved in fuel. It may however be worth double-glazing the windows in the main living-room. Thick, lined curtains are a much less expensive but very effective way of reducing heat loss.

5 Floors and chimneys

Thick carpets and underlays save heat. Unused fireplaces can be blocked but should be partly ventilated to prevent condensation in the chimney.

6 The hot water tank

Much of the cost of water heating can be saved by lagging the tank with a jacket at least 75 mm (3″) thick. This is easy to fit and cheap – it could pay for itself in two or three months. Most modern houses are supplied with lagged tanks. It is wasteful to leave the tank unlagged just to provide an airing cupboard. Some tanks are available with insulation already fitted.

Hot water pipes should be lagged, and cold pipes also need insulating to prevent freezing in winter.

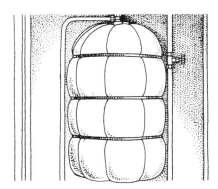

Questions

1 **Why should you insulate your home as well as possible?**
2 **Describe how and why you would insulate your loft.**
3 **How could you get rid of draughts?**
4 **How does cavity-wall insulation work?**
5 **How would you choose a firm to insulate the cavity walls in your home?**
6 **Double glazing is very expensive. Suggest another way of reducing the heat loss through windows.**
7 **What are the advantages of double glazing?**
8 **Why should a hot water tank be well lagged?**
9 **What is the best way to do this?**

Ventilation

Ventilation means exchanging the stale air in a room for fresh air. If the air in a room remained still and unchanged the room would soon feel stuffy and uncomfortable, and it would make you feel tired.

When you ventilate a room, you remove the stale air which contains uncomfortable amounts of moisture, smoke, steam, warmth and carbon dioxide, and replace it with fresh air.

Ventilation is helped by the natural upward movement of currents of warm air which are replaced by cooler air. It is important to try to introduce fresh air into a room without causing draughts.

There are several different methods of ventilating a room:

1 A coal fire

Hot air rises up the chimney and cool air is drawn from the room to replace it. Although this method provides good ventilation, it can often feel very draughty to the people in the room.

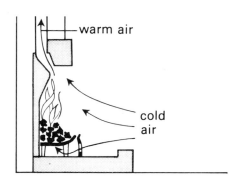

2 Doors and windows

Open doors and windows provide ventilation. Where a small window can be left open at the top, fresh air can be brought into the room without causing a draught.

3 Electric air fresheners

These are plugged into a socket and remove tobacco smoke and other cooking and household smells by means of an electric fan. They work quite effectively, are quiet in use and inexpensive to buy.

4 Cooker hoods

These are fitted above the hob of cookers, usually in a fitted kitchen (see page 106). They remove steam, grease, and cooking smells from the kitchen by means of an electric fan. The fan draws in the polluted air and either passes it outside through a duct, or passes it through a deodorizing carbon filter and recirculates it. The hoods have a built-in light and some can have a 'decor' panel fitted to match the rest of the cupboard fronts in the kitchen.

5 Extractor fan

This can be set in the window. It works electrically and draws stale air and cooking smells out of the kitchen. It is fairly expensive to install and is rather noisy in use.

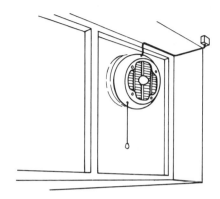

6 A Cooper's disc

This is inserted in a window and may be turned to the open or the closed position.

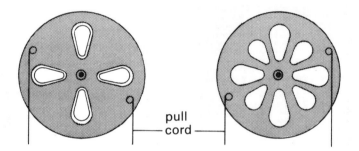

pull
cord

7 Air conditioning

This is a complete system which controls both the temperature and the humidity (moisture content) of the air being circulated around a building. Air-conditioning systems are not built into houses in this country but are widely used in modern office blocks, factories and large stores.

Questions

1 **Why is it necessary to ventilate rooms?**
2 **How does a coal fire ventilate a room?**
3 **What is the disadvantage of ventilating a room by means of a coal fire?**
4 **Describe a method of ventilation which would be suitable for:**
 a a living-room
 b a bathroom
 c a kitchen
 d a department store.

Lighting

Good lighting in the home is important. It helps to prevent eye-strain and accidents, and to create a cheerful, homely atmosphere.

The best, most even kind of light is natural sunlight. The amount of sunlight a room receives will depend on the position and size of the windows.

Artificial light is provided by electricity. It is easy to use and control, and it is inexpensive.

Different kinds of lighting are suitable for different areas of the house. A kitchen needs to be well lit, and for this fluorescent strip lighting is particularly suitable. It is economical to run and provides good light with no shadows. A 100 or 150 watt bulb is suitable for the centre light in a room. 60 watt bulbs can be used for table lamps, spotlights, and floor standing lamps, to provide extra light for close work such as reading or sewing.

Light fittings

Light fittings are used to avoid the harsh glare of the light bulb and to produce different effects.

1   *Direct lighting* The bulb is covered by a shade which sends all the light downwards. This is most suitable for close work.

2   *Indirect lighting* The bulb is completely concealed by the shade and the light is reflected up to the ceiling and on to the walls. This is most suitable for wall lights and halls.

3   *General lighting* The bulb is enclosed in a translucent fitting, and light is sent out in all directions. This is suitable for all rooms.

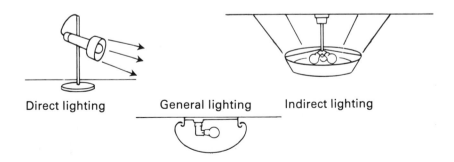

Direct lighting   General lighting   Indirect lighting

A pendant light in the centre of the room gives more light than wall lights of the same wattage. Table lamps and floor-standing lamps can provide extra lighting around the room. Spotlights can be directed on to pictures or ornaments, and a lighting track allows you to move spotlights to highlight different areas of the room. In the dining-room, a 'rise-and-fall' fitment can be used over the table.

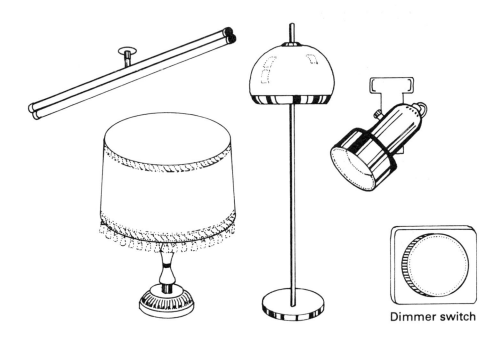

Dimmer switch

Economy in lighting

Although lighting costs make up only a small proportion of the electricity bill (most of the cost goes on heating and hot water), some economies can still be made to reduce lighting costs.

1 Lights can be switched off when not in use, but for safety the stairs should always be well lit.
2 Soft general lighting with work areas more brightly lit is better and cheaper than bright lighting for the whole room.
3 Dimmer switches can be used to reduce the amount of lighting required. This is both economical and attractive.
4 Low wattage bulbs, e.g. 40W, 60W, can safely be used in the bedrooms, bathroom and W.C.
5 Coloured shades can be changed for lighter shades which give out more light.
6 Fluorescent lights are cheaper to run.
7 A new type of bulb is available which gives the same amount of light as an ordinary bulb, but uses less electricity. It lasts much longer than an ordinary bulb, but is expensive to buy in the first place.

Questions

1 **How are light fittings used to produce**
(a) direct, (b) indirect, and (c) general lighting?
For which areas of the house is each suitable?
2 **Suggest a plan for producing suitable and attractive lighting for**
(a) a living/dining-room, (b) a kitchen, and (c) a hall.
Give reasons for your suggestions.
3 **Name some safe ways of reducing the cost of lighting.**

Further work on chapter 3

1 Your bedroom is going to be decorated and you can choose some new light fittings. At present there is just one central pendant light. Work out and cost the kind of lighting you would like to install.

2 You have to go on a course for four months in the winter and are staying in lodgings. Your room only has one small central heating radiator and is very cold. What could you do to improve matters?

3 Your kitchen at home gets very steamed up and damp. What could you suggest that would bring about an improvement?

4 Your family has just moved into an older three-bedroomed house with no central heating. Your parents have decided to have it installed. What useful suggestions could you make?

5 Find out what you can about the use of solar energy and heat exchangers in the home for heating and hot water.

Sources of further information

British Gas Education Service and The Electricity Council (addresses on page 52). Gas and electricity showrooms have leaflets on heaters, fires, central heating methods, saving energy, and other subjects.

Department of Energy (address on page 52) publishes several free booklets including one called 'A Guide to Home Heating Costs' which compares the cost of heating a variety of sizes of home by different methods. Also 'Handy Hints to Help You at Home' and 'Reducing Home Energy Costs.'

Films
Concord Films Council Ltd. (address page 52) have films and videos on energy, including solar energy and energy conservation.

Guild Sound and Vision, 6 Royce Road, Peterborough, PE1 5YB, on cavity wall insulation.

Computer software
'Central heating (homes)' on heat loss and insulation. Heinemann Software, The Windmill Press, Kingswood, Tadworth, Surrey K20 6TG.

Chapter 4

Furniture and furnishings

Room planning

Choosing colour schemes and furnishings for a room so that it looks really attractive is much more difficult than it appears. You should spend a lot of time on careful planning before making any final choice, if you want a good effect.

Any mistake you make, such as choosing the wrong colour carpet, can be so expensive that you will have to live with it for a long time, even though it irritates you every time you look at it.

When you plan and furnish any room you will nearly always have to keep certain items – it is not very often that you can buy everything new. Always take these furnishings into account when you choose colours and patterns for your new scheme.

Planning any room involves: choice of decorations; furniture; carpets; curtains and soft furnishings; and lighting.

Colour schemes

The most important factor in deciding whether or not a room looks well planned is colour. If you can choose the colours of everything in the room so that they look good together, then you are well on the way to having an attractive room.

Getting colours to match and blend to give the effect you want is not easy and does not often happen by accident. It is very useful if you know a little bit about colour before you start.

The three main colours are red, yellow and blue. By mixing and blending these three you can make up most other colours.

Look carefully at the colour wheel on the back cover and you will see how the other colours are produced as these three gradually blend together.

Choosing colours which go well together
1 Use the colour wheel to help you choose colours which will go well together, and to avoid a clash.
2 Avoid placing colours from opposite sides of the wheel beside each other, as the contrast between them will tend to be vivid and harsh. Examples of this are orange and blue, or red and green.
3 Colours which are fairly close on the wheel will give a softer, more pleasant contrast, as they blend together naturally.

Other points about colour
1 Some colours give a warm feeling to a room, for example, red, orange, and yellow. They can brighten up a room which does not get much natural sunlight.
2 Other colours create a cool, restful atmosphere in a room, for example, blue and green. They would be suitable for a room which had plenty of sunlight.
3 *Neutrals* such as white, cream, grey or black are not really colours. They will link your colour scheme together.
4 Several different shades of the same colour can be used together. A shade is a lighter or darker version of the same colour.

Choosing your colour scheme

1 The main colour should be chosen first – choose one you really like and will not tire of too quickly, and which is either warm or cool to suit the room.

2 A neutral colour should be chosen next to link the scheme together, for example, white, cream or grey.

3 A contrasting colour in small amounts gives interest. This may come from opposite your main colour on the wheel for a vivid, lively contrast, or from nearer to the main colour on the wheel for a softer, less startling, contrast. This colour could be used for lamp shades, cushions or rugs.

4 Plan around any furnishings or carpet you have to keep and always fit them into any new scheme.

5 The most expensive items are probably the carpet and armchairs. If these are chosen in a neutral shade you will be able to change your colour scheme quite simply when you feel like it, by changing the colours used for smaller items, like cushions, lamps or an alcove wall.

Texture

Texture can be brought into your scheme to make surfaces look more interesting. Texture means the way a material or surface <u>feels</u> when you touch it. A very smooth material like cotton has no texture but a material with a raised pile or weave, such as rough tweed, velvet, or a long-pile carpet has texture. It will look and feel more interesting than a smooth, flat material.

Pattern

Some pattern in a room provides interest and is useful for hiding marks and general wear and tear. Too much pattern in any room will make it look cluttered and busy. As a general rule, <u>never</u> have more than one large pattern in a room. If, for example, you choose a highly patterned carpet to hide the usual marks of family wear, you should avoid having a vividly patterned wallpaper or curtains as well. A very small, neat, overall pattern could be used as well, though, and could look very attractive.

Matching wallpaper and material for curtains, cushion covers or bedspreads can be bought in some very attractive designs.

Questions

1 **What effect do colours from opposite each other on the wheel give when placed together?**

2 **Name three pairs of colours which show this rather harsh contrast.**

3 **What effect do colours near each other on the wheel give when placed together?**

4 **Suggest three pairs of colours which you think would give a pleasing contrast in a room.**

5 **List the five most important rules to remember when planning a colour scheme.**

6 **Plan a colour scheme for a bedroom for yourself, following the rules given above. Say what colours you would use for a carpet, the walls, a bedspread, the curtains and the lampshades. Where would you bring in some pattern and texture?**

7 **Suggest a scheme suitable for a family living-room.**

Choosing furniture

Furniture should be very carefully chosen as it is expensive and receives a lot of hard wear. As the cost is so high, it may suit you to buy new furniture on hire-purchase (see page 152). If a piece of furniture is well made it will stay in good condition long after it has been paid for, but if it is of poor quality it will soon look shabby.

Good second-hand furniture from sales or friends may be a better buy than badly-made new items. It can be improved with new paint and covers and can be replaced later when you can afford it.

Furniture discount centres (for example MFI) sell furniture in 'flat-packs' ready to assemble at home. You have to be quite experienced at 'do-it-yourself' to make a good job of this, but the furniture is less expensive, is attractive, and of reasonable quality for the price. It also saves you having to wait, perhaps weeks, for delivery.

Points to consider before buying any furniture

1 Which pieces do you really need?
2 Is it solidly made?
3 Will it be easily marked?
4 How should you clean or polish it?
5 Will it match the rest of your furniture?
6 What will it look like after a couple of years of family use?
7 How long must you wait for delivery?
8 What can you afford to pay, in cash or by hire-purchase?
9 Can you buy the same item more cheaply at a furniture discount warehouse?
10 Does it have a Design Centre label?

Look for the Design Centre label attached to furniture. It shows that it has been selected by the Council of Industrial Design as being a well-designed article. That is, it is of good quality, well made for its purpose and attractive in appearance.

Choosing particular pieces of furniture

Tables
1 The table should be large enough for all the family. Some can have an extra leaf added, and others fold down when not in use.
2 It should be steady and should not wobble. Check this carefully with a 'drop-leaf' folding table.
3 The finish is important. It should be fairly resistant to scratches and heat. Most tables need protection against hot plates by table mats.
4 Tables with Formica or Melamine tops are popular for daily use as they are resistant to heat and scratches and they can be washed.

Chairs
1 Dining chairs should be firm and support the back comfortably.
2 Easily cleaned chairs are needed when there are children who may spill food.
3 The chairs should be the right height for the table with which they are used.

Sideboard
1 This can be useful for storing cutlery, table cloths and other items.
2 It should have plenty of drawer and cupboard space.
3 If it is a suitable height it can be used for serving meals.

Armchairs and settees
1 They should be comfortable. A high back gives more support to the head than a low back.
2 The frame and cushions should be firmly made but not too heavy.
3 The cover should be firmly woven to stand up to daily use.
4 The colour should be practical so that it will not show every mark.
5 A three-piece suite is not always the best choice. Individual chairs may suit the family better.
6 A settee which converts to a bed may be useful for visitors.

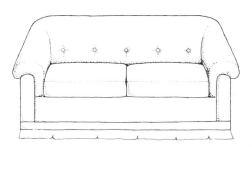
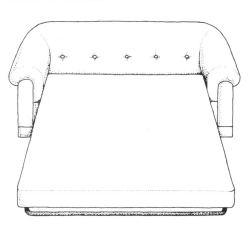

Beds

1 As you spend about one-third of your life in bed, you should buy the best you can afford. The standard widths are 150 cms for a double bed, 100 cms for a single. The length is 200 cms.

2 Bunk beds save a lot of space in a smaller home, but they are often only 75 cms wide.

3 Modern beds are divans, consisting of a base which should be really firm, and a mattress. You may prefer either a firm or a soft mattress. Always lie down on the mattress to test it before you buy.

4 Mattresses may be filled with foam or springs. A good foam mattress is firm and comfortable, does not need turning and does not make dust.

5 Spring mattresses vary in quality. The best are usually the most expensive but they will stay comfortable for much longer. They contain individually pocketed springs. There may be up to 2000 inside a double mattress.

6 Headboards are sold separately from the divan bed. They should be firm enough to take the weight of someone leaning against them. They can be very attractive and may be made of wood, Dralon velvet, brass or cane.

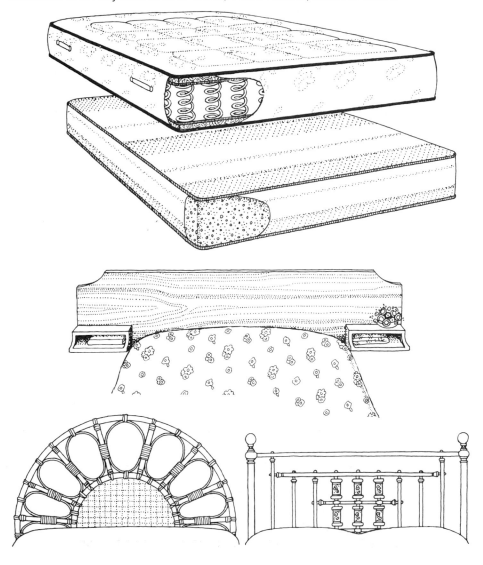

Wardrobes
1 Wardrobes should be deep enough for a coat hanger and tall enough for a long dress. Shelves inside may be useful.
2 Fitted wardrobes, often combined with a dressing-table and chest of drawers, are popular. They can be fixed to the wall, reaching to the ceiling, so they provide plenty of storage space and avoid dust collecting on top.

Chest of drawers
1 The drawers should be firmly made, preferably with corners 'dove-tailed' rather than glued.

2 They should fit well, run smoothly, and be smoothly finished inside.
3 Handles should be comfortable and easy to hold.

Dressing-table
1 There should be a good mirror and a shallow drawer for cosmetics.
2 The surface should not be too easily marked by spilt perfume or make-up.
3 Make sure there is enough space below for your knees, so that you can sit comfortably.

Questions
1 **How can a young couple make their money go as far as possible when they are buying furniture?**
2 **What do you think are the four most important points to consider when choosing any furniture, and why?**
3 **What furniture do you think is necessary for (a) a living-room with a dining area at one end, and (b) a bedroom?**
4 **What must you look out for when choosing (a) a table and chairs, (b) armchairs, (c) a bed, (d) a wardrobe, (e) a chest of drawers, and (f) a dressing-table?**
5 **Draw the Design Centre label and explain what it means.**

Materials used to make furniture

Wood

Hardwood
For example, teak, mahogany, oak. These trees take a long time to grow so their wood is expensive, but firm and hard-wearing. It is used to make good, solid furniture or to make veneers, and is attractive to look at.

Veneers are extremely thin layers of attractive, good quality wood stuck on to the front of furniture made from cheaper, softer wood to improve its appearance.

Softwood
For example, pine and spruce. It grows more quickly and so is less hard-wearing, but cheaper. It is used to make the base of veneered furniture and to make unpainted whitewood furniture. Solid pine furniture is popular and attractive but gets marked more easily than a solid hardwood such as teak.

Chipboard
This is made by treating wood with resins. It is used to make a lot of modern, inexpensive furniture. The chipboard is finished with either:

a a veneer of better quality wood.
b a plastic such as Formica or Melamine, often with a white or wood-grain finish. This is used in kitchen furniture and 'unit' furniture for bedrooms and living-rooms. It is fairly cheap, it can be cleaned by washing, and it resists heat and scratches.

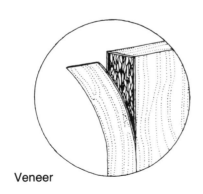

Veneer

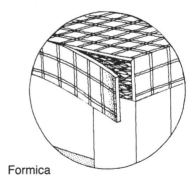

Formica

Other materials

Metal e.g. chrome – for arms and legs of tables and chairs.

Plastic can be moulded to make lightweight, easily cleaned chairs and tables.

Leather is expensive, attractive and hard-wearing. Imitation leather or P.V.C. is much cheaper, fairly hard-wearing and easy to clean.

Dralon is used for armchairs and settees. It has a soft, velvety appearance, but is tough and easily shampooed.

Fires

Many fires have been caused by armchairs and settees being set alight by matches or cigarettes. New furniture which could burn easily has this swing label attached to it to warn against this danger.

How to look after wood surfaces

Wood in its natural state is easily marked, so it has to have a 'finish' or seal. This may be one of the following:

Finish on the wood	*How to clean and care for it*
Cellulose Used on tables, chairs, school desks. Not easily marked.	Remove marks with damp cloth, dry. Polish occasionally. Protect from heat.
Teak veneer or *solid teak* Used for bedroom/dining-room furniture.	Do not polish. Rub with teak oil about three times a year.
French polish Used on older, expensive furniture. Gives a high gloss. Easily marked by heat and scratches.	Remove marks with warm, damp cloth. Dry well. Polish with furniture cream. Protect from heat.
Wax The original polish for wood. Used on old oak furniture and pine.	Use wax polish sparingly. Rub well to bring out shine.
Paint Mainly used for kitchen and nursery furniture.	Wash with warm soapy water. Rinse and dry well.
Plastic laminates e.g. Formica. Widely used for cheaper furniture and for kitchens.	Can be washed and dried frequently without harm. Resists heat and scratches.

Questions

1 **Name three hardwoods. Why are they expensive?**
2 **How are hardwoods used in furniture?**
3 **What is a veneer?**
4 **What kind of furniture is often made from softwood?**
5 **Name some pieces of furniture often made from chipboard.**
6 **What are the advantages of chipboard furniture?**
7 **How would you care for the following to keep them in good condition?**
   a a Formica-topped bench in the kitchen.
   b a teak dining-table
   c a white painted cupboard in a child's bedroom.
   d the wooden arms and legs of an easy chair.

Carpets

Buying carpets can be very expensive. Always go to a shop where you can trust the assistant to give you good advice. Most carpets look attractive when they are new, but you need other information if you want to know how they will look after a few years' use.

Grades of carpet

Always look for the labels attached to carpets, which tell you how hard-wearing you can expect the carpets to be. These are the grades you will find:

Light domestic – for bedrooms only, where there is very little wear.

Medium domestic – where there is only a little more wear, e.g. in a dining-room which is not in everyday use.

General domestic – suitable for anywhere in the house.

Heavy domestic – very good for areas receiving a lot of wear, e.g. hall or living-room.

Luxury domestic – luxurious and hard-wearing, it can be used anywhere.

Underlay

A good underlay makes carpets last much longer and feel softer and thicker. It also helps keep heat in the room. It is made from thick felt, or foam rubber with a special backing.

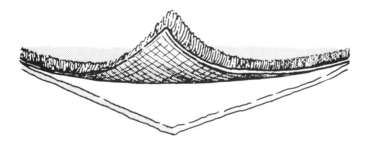

Many cheaper carpets have a built-in foam underlay to make them softer and longer-lasting. A layer of specially thick paper should always be laid between this kind of carpeting and the floor below, or the foam may stick to the floor and tear when you try to lift it.

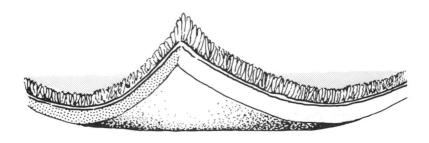

Points to remember when choosing carpets

The colour
The colour should tone in with the rest of the furnishings in the room. Dark colours show threads and crumbs, very light colours are easily marked.

The pattern
A plain carpet will show every mark. A very vivid pattern will not show marks, but you may soon get tired of it. Too many patterns in a room, on the carpet, curtains, walls and cushions, look cluttered and unattractive.

Fitted carpet, square or tiles?
Fitted carpets are expensive, but are easy to clean and give a spacious, luxurious look to a room.

A carpet square is less expensive. It can easily be moved to a different room or house and can be turned around to help it wear more evenly or to hide a stain.

Tiles are easy to lay and fit. Any worn or marked square can be moved to where it will not show.

Caring for your carpet

New carpets
Some carpets shed fluff when new. You should leave them to 'settle' for a couple of months and clean them with a sweeper or brush, not a vacuum cleaner. Later, vacuum two or three times a week, and sweep or brush in between.

Shampoo
Choose a suitable pattern and colour and you will not have to shampoo too often. Nylon and acrylic carpets are easy to shampoo and quick to dry, but attract dirt more than a wool carpet.

Use a foam carpet shampoo. A vacuum cleaner will remove the dirt and shampoo together when the carpet dries. Choose a warm day and do not get the carpet too wet. Let it dry completely before putting the furniture back.

Questions

1 **List the five grades of carpet. For which part of the house is each one suitable?**
2 **How can you find out what grade a carpet is when you are in a shop?**
3 **Which grade would you expect to be (a) cheapest, and (b) most expensive?**
4 **How would you expect the carpet to wear if you put (a) a medium domestic in the living-room, (b) a light domestic in the hall, and (c) a general domestic in the dining-room?**
5 **What are the advantages of having a good underlay?**
6 **How must you prepare the floor before laying a foam-backed carpet? Why?**
7 **What must you remember when choosing the pattern and colour of a carpet?**
8 **What are the good and bad points of a carpet square?**

How carpets are made

The way in which a carpet can be expected to last, without becoming worn and shabby, depends on two main points:

1 The construction of the carpet (the way it is made).
2 The fibre it is made from.

The construction of carpets

The terms 'Axminster', 'Wilton', 'tufted' and 'corded' apply to the way the carpet is made, not to who makes it, or what it is made from.

Axminster and Wilton

These are both woven carpets. The pile and the backing are woven together in a way which produces a firm, well-made carpet.

If an Axminster or Wilton is made of 100% wool, or 80% wool and 20% nylon, the carpet will be top quality, luxurious in appearance and hard-wearing.

But if an Axminster or Wilton is made of a mixture of rayon and wool, then the carpet will be of lower quality, perhaps suitable only for medium domestic use.

The terms Axminster and Wilton, then, do not always mean that a carpet is of the best quality. The quality also depends on the fibre used.

The difference between an Axminster and a Wilton is in the way they are woven. An Axminster can include more colours and pattern than a Wilton, which can only have up to three colours and a simpler pattern, though the carpet may be slightly thicker.

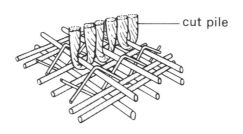

cut pile

Tufted carpets

These have the backing produced first, then the pile stitched into it. A further backing is then added, often of foam rubber, to keep it firm. Tufted carpets are made of various fibres and are fairly inexpensive, but they are not as firm and hard-wearing as good woven carpets.

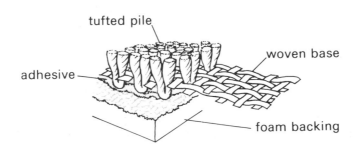

tufted pile

woven base

adhesive

foam backing

Cord carpets

These are woven in a similar way to Axminster and Wilton, with a firm, tight loop. They have no pile and are usually very hard-wearing, depending on the fibre used (often hair or sisal). They are not soft to touch, being firm and rather hard, but they provide an attractive, long-lasting fitted carpet at a very reasonable price.

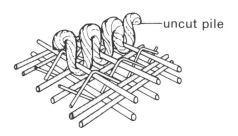
—uncut pile

The fibres used to make carpets

Carpets are made mainly from wool, nylon, acrylic and rayon. The fibre used is very important in deciding how long the carpet will wear.

1 *Wool* is usually accepted as being the best fibre. Up to 20% nylon is sometimes added for extra strength. It is warm, thick, soft and resilient (it will not flatten in use). It does not get dirty easily but it is expensive.

2 *Acrylic* Brand names include Acrilan and Courtelle. Acrylic is more like wool than any other man-made fibre, being warm, resilient and soft. It attracts dirt more easily than wool, but is easier to clean and less expensive.

3 *Nylon* Brand names include Bri-nylon and Enkalon. Strong and hard-wearing, it attracts dirt, but is easy to shampoo and dries quickly. It is suitable for use in a kitchen. It does not feel as soft and warm to touch as wool.

4 *Rayon* Brand names include Evlan. This is not a resilient fibre so the pile soon flattens. It picks up dirt easily. Its advantage is its low cost, but it does not wear well. It is often mixed with wool or other fibres to make them cheaper.

Questions
1 **Name three different methods used to manufacture carpets.**
2 **What are the two main factors which decide how hard-wearing a carpet will be?**
3 **What is the difference between an Axminster and a Wilton?**
4 **Is an Axminster always a best quality carpet? Why is this?**
5 **What are the good and bad points of (a) a tufted carpet, and (b) a cord carpet?**
6 **What are the fibres most often used to make carpets?**
7 **What are (a) the advantages, and (b) the disadvantages of each of these fibres?**

Curtains

Choosing the material

1 Look for a colour and pattern which will go with the rest of the furnishings in the room.
2 Ask if the material can be washed, either by hand or machine. If it has to be dry-cleaned, this is much more expensive.
3 Many curtain materials shrink in the wash. You should ask about this before you buy, and allow extra length to let the hem down if necessary after washing.
4 Ask if the material is colour-fast, or whether the colours will run into each other when the curtains are washed. This is especially important when there are several different colours in the material.

Making the curtains

You can choose whether to have your curtains reaching to the window sill, just below the sill or to the floor.

If you have radiators below the window, never cover them with long curtains or they will not warm the room and the curtains may be spoilt by being so close to the radiator.

Measuring is important to make sure you buy the right amount of material so that the curtains will hang attractively. You must allow at least 1½ times the width of the curtain track if the curtain is to look full enough. If for example the curtain track is 300 cm wide you need 450 cm of material across the top.

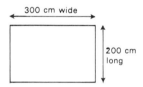

Curtain material is usually about 120 cm wide so you will need four 'drops' or curtains which will give you 4 × 120 cm = 480 cm width (or 4 m 80 cm). 25 cm of material has to be added to the length of each 'drop' or curtain, to allow for the hem, the heading, and in case of shrinkage. So for the window in the diagram above you would have to add 4 × 25 = 100 cm for the four curtain lengths.

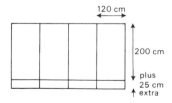

The amount of material you would need altogether would therefore be 4 × 225 cm = 900 cm = 9 metres.

Lining

It is a good idea to line curtains, because:

1   It stops the curtains fading in the sun.
2   It makes them hang better and look fuller.
3   It helps keep the heat inside the room and the cold air out.

The linings can be sewn into the curtains or they can be detachable to make it easier to wash them.

Ready-made curtains

These can be bought to fit most windows. This is quite a lot more expensive than making your own, but it does ensure that the curtains are well made and attractive.

Venetian blinds

These can be used instead of curtains, or as well as curtains to give privacy. When they are open, people in the room can see out but no one can see inside. However, they are expensive to buy, awkward to clean and they look rather bare without curtains as well.

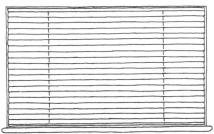

Roller blinds

These can be bought or made from do-it-yourself kits, in many attractive patterns. They are less expensive than Venetian blinds, though not as long-lasting. They work on a spring and can be 'set' in any position.

Questions

1   **What are the most important points to remember when buying curtain material?**
2   **How much curtain material 120 cm wide would you need for a window (a) 200 cm wide × 175 cm deep, (b) 480 cm wide × 225 cm deep?**
3   **Why is it a good idea to line your curtains?**
4   **Ready-made curtains are fairly expensive but they have several advantages. List as many as you can think of.**

Choosing bedding

Sheets

Sheets should be big enough for your bed, so that they will stay tucked in properly.

For the standard single bed 100 cm wide, the sheets should be about 175 cm × 260 cm.
For the standard double bed 150 cm wide, the sheets should be about 230 cm × 260 cm.

Fitted sheets
You can buy pairs of 'fitted' sheets where the bottom sheet is elasticated, fits tightly around the mattress and cannot come undone. The top sheet is fitted only at the foot of the bed and can be folded back over the blankets. The disadvantage of these fitted sheets is that their position cannot be changed around from top to bottom as a flat sheet can.

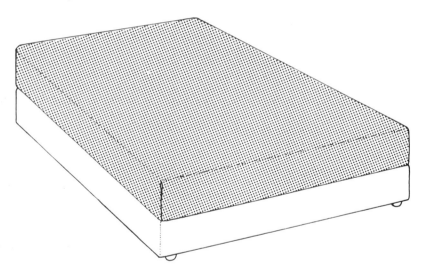

Materials
The most popular materials for making sheets are cotton, flannelette, polyester and cotton, and nylon.

Cotton sheets feel cool and comfortable. Good quality cotton is very hard-wearing. These sheets need ironing, are usually available in plain colours only and are rather expensive.

Flannelette or brushed cotton sheets feel soft and warm to the touch when you get into bed. They tend to be less hard-wearing than smooth cotton.

Polyester and cotton mixture. These are available in many attractive colours and patterns. They feel quite smooth to the touch and are less expensive than pure cotton. They are easy to wash, quick to dry and need very little ironing.

Nylon sheets are quite cheap but many people find them uncomfortable to sleep in as they are not absorbent. They are very easy to wash, quick to dry and need no ironing. They can be smooth or have a warmer, brushed finish.

Pillowcases

Pillowcases are available to match most sheets and are usually sold in pairs. The normal size is 50 cm × 75 cm.

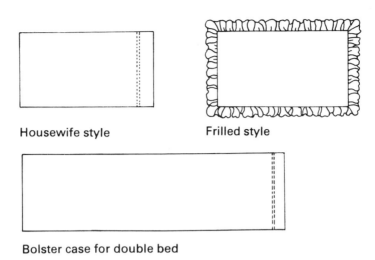

Housewife style

Frilled style

Bolster case for double bed

You should always use an extra pillowslip between the pillow and the pillowcase, to keep the pillow itself really clean.

Blankets

Blankets can be bought with plain hems, or with the ends bound, in many attractive colours. Cellular woven blankets are warm as they trap pockets of warm air.

Blankets are usually made of:

a *Wool.* Warm and hard-wearing, these are the best blankets. Check to see if they are machine-washable and moth-proofed.

b *Acrylic fibre.* These include Acrilan and Courtelle. They are easily washed and dried, moths will not attack them and they are less expensive than wool.

c *Viscose fibre.* These are the cheapest blankets. They are less warm and do not wash very well as they flatten. Buy better quality if you can. One wool blanket will be warmer and last longer than two poor quality blankets.

Eiderdowns

Eiderdowns can be as warm as two or three blankets. They can be filled with down or feathers, or if filled with Terylene or other man-made fibres they can be easily washed and dried.

Bedspreads

Bedspreads make the bed look tidy, and keep the dust off the bedding. They should match the colour scheme of the room. There are many attractive materials to choose from, such as candlewick, cotton or quilted nylon.

Continental quilts (duvets)

These are lightweight quilts with a special filling, used instead of blankets and other bed-covers.

They are popular as they have many advantages:

1   They are very warm in winter and cool in summer.
2   They make bed-making very quick and easy, as they only need to be shaken and replaced.
3   They do not create dust and fluff.
4   You only need the quilt in its cover over you, cutting out the need for a top sheet, blankets, eiderdown and bedspread.
5   You can buy very attractive matching covers, bottom sheets, valances and pillowcases, in many colours and patterns.
6   As you do not have to buy blankets and other bed-covers, they are not too expensive to buy and they last a very long time.

The quilt can be filled with any of these fillings:

a   *Pure down* – very soft, light, warm and expensive. Down is the fine soft underfeathers of ducks or other birds.

b   *Feathers and down mixed* – this mixture is most often chosen. Neither down nor feathers can be washed or cleaned.

c   *Terylene P3* –a special fibre produced for quilts. It is washable, so it is the most suitable choice of filling for children.

It is important that the quilt is about 45 cm wider than the bed it is for, so that there will be an overlap on both sides.

Continental quilts have a 'tog' rating which indicates how warm you can expect the quilt to be. The tog rating ranges from 7.5 to 13.5 togs. The higher the tog rating, the warmer the quilt. Look for the B.S.I. Kitemark when you go to buy a quilt.

Pillows

Pillows can be filled with down, feathers, Terylene or foam rubber. The more expensive the pillow, the longer it will usually stay comfortable. You need two pillows for a single bed and four pillows or a bolster and two pillows for a double bed.

Towels

Towels can be bought in many attractive colours to match the colour scheme in your bathroom. Darker shades have to be washed on their own several times as the colour can run.

Towels vary in size:

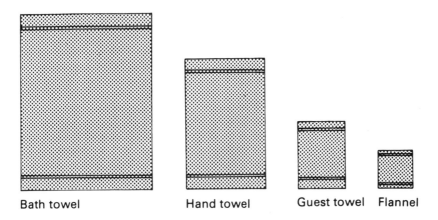

Bath towel   Hand towel   Guest towel   Flannel

Questions

1 **What size should sheets and blankets be to fit (a) a single bed, and (b) a double bed?**
2 **What are the points for and against buying fitted sheets for all your beds?**
3 **Name four materials often used to make sheets. What are the advantages and disadvantages of each one?**
4 **What kind of blankets are usually (a) the warmest, (b) the cheapest, (c) the most easily machine-washed, (d) liable to be attacked by moths, and (e) the most expensive?**
5 **Give as many reasons as you can why many people buy continental quilts rather than blankets and other bed-covers.**
6 **Name a filling suitable for a continental quilt for a 4-year-old child.**
7 **What special care must you take when washing a new set of dark-coloured bath towels?**

Keeping your home clean

A house which is clean, tidy and well cared for is always a good background for family life. The more efficiently you can plan and carry out your housework, the more time you will have free to enjoy the company of your family and to follow your other interests and hobbies.

The amount of time you spend on housework will depend on:

1 How well organized you are.
2 Whether you and your family are at home, school or work all day.
3 How much you enjoy or dislike housework.
4 How much help you have from labour-saving appliances or from other people.

Daily routines

A couple who both work

When a couple both have jobs, they will share the work of running the home between them, in the way that suits them best. Perhaps one will cook the evening meal and the other will wash up afterwards. At the weekend perhaps one will wash and iron and the other will dust and vacuum. They might do the weekly shopping together.

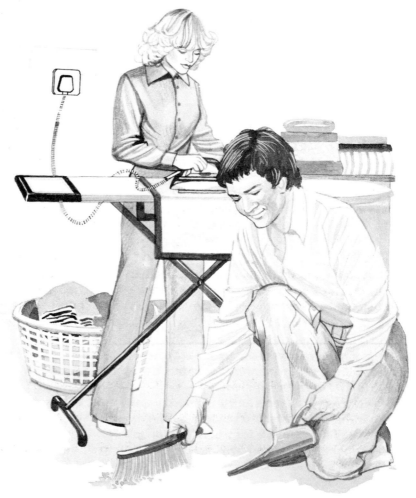

The way in which they divide the work doesn't matter. The important thing is to realize that both should have a fair share of work and leisure time.

One person at home all day

When one person is at home all day, perhaps with small children, he/she will probably do most of the routine housework during the day. However, when babies are very small and when two- or three-year-olds are at the very energetic stage, they need constant attention. There may be very little time to spare for extra housework in between cooking meals, washing up, shopping and washing clothes.

The other partner can help in various ways. When a baby is very young both partners can take turns in getting up when the baby wakes up at night. They can both bath children and put them to bed in the evening. By sharing the daily routine like this both partners will get to know their children better, and will each have their fair share of leisure in the evening.

Labour-saving equipment

An automatic washing machine is a great time-saver in a family with children. With babies in the family the number of dirty nappies to be washed can seem endless. Babies may need several changes of clothes in a day, and small children playing on the floor or outside in the garden or yard can get very grubby very quickly. They may need clean, dry clothes at least once a day. Older children playing football or climbing trees or walls will add to the pile of washing. A washing machine is more of a necessity than a luxury in these circumstances, and non-iron clothes which can be machine-washed are the most sensible choice.

Children helping at home

Children should be encouraged to be useful members of the family from an early age. Even small children can put toys away, and tidy their beds, especially if they have continental quilts. They can help clear and lay the table. Older children and teenagers can help with cooking, washing, cleaning, and shopping. They should all be able to iron their own shirts and press their own trousers.

If everyone helps in the running of the household then all the members of the family will realize that hot meals don't just appear on the table and that clean, ironed clothes don't just appear in the drawer.

If someone always waits hand and foot on the family, they cannot be surprised if the work is taken for granted rather than being appreciated. Nor is it any help to children if they grow up incapable of looking after themselves when they leave home.

Questions

1 **Do you think it is a good idea to do the housework according to a routine? Why is this?**
2 **What are the factors which decide how much time you spend on housework every day?**
3 **Suggest a possible routine for a young couple with no children, who both leave for work at 8.30 a.m. and return about 5.30 p.m.**

Cleaning routines

There are some jobs in the house which have to be done every day to keep the house looking tidy and clean. Other jobs should be done at least weekly, to keep the home thoroughly clean. There are extra household jobs too, which have to be fitted in when necessary.

How often you do these extra jobs, for example cleaning mirrors and windows, washing ornaments, washing curtains and walls, shampooing carpets and chairs, depends on you. Some people enjoy housework, others hate it, most people are somewhere in between. Everyone decides for himself or herself how important it is to them whether or not the furniture is always immaculately polished and completely free of dust. Often people would rather spend their spare time doing something they find more interesting and enjoyable.

It is important, however, to have high standards of cleanliness in the kitchen and bathroom, because these are areas where bacteria could thrive and cause illness. Nobody wants to eat food which has been prepared in a dirty kitchen, and nobody wants to use a bathroom or toilet which isn't clean.

To clean rooms thoroughly you should work in this order:

Kitchen

1 Open the window to air the room.
2 Thoroughly wash and dry the sink and draining-board.
3 Clean the cooker, including the oven. This is much easier if the cooker is wiped down each time it is used.
4 Wash work surfaces with hot, soapy water.
5 Defrost and clean the refrigerator.
6 Clean the larder or food cupboard.
7 Wipe the paintwork, cupboard doors and window sills.
8 Empty and wash the waste bin.
9 Sweep and wash the floor.

Living-room

1 Open the windows.
2 Clean and lay the coal fire if there is one.
3 Empty the ashtrays and waste-paper basket, remove old newspapers or dead flowers.
4 Tidy the room, straighten cushions.
5 Sweep or vacuum the carpet and surrounds.
6 Dust and polish the furniture.
7 Dust the skirting boards, wipe the paintwork with a damp cloth.
8 Vacuum or brush the chairs.

Bedrooms

1 Open the windows.
2 Tidy away clothes, toys and books.
3 Make the beds – everyone in the family should make their own bed.
4 Change the sheets when necessary.
5 Sweep or vacuum the carpet.
6 Dust and polish or wash the furniture.
7 Wipe the paintwork.

Bathroom

1 Open the window, straighten the towels.
2 Brush the W.C. with a special lavatory brush.
3 Wash the lavatory with a mild solution of disinfectant. You should keep a special cloth for cleaning the W.C. and not use it for any other job.
4 Encourage everyone to clean the bath straight after use, when it is much easier to do. Use a little detergent or a non-scratch cleaner which will not spoil the surface. Never use harsh scouring powder.
5 Clean the wash basin with the same cleaner. Rinse it well.
6 Wipe under and around the taps with a damp cloth, then rub them dry.
7 Wipe the window sill to remove dust.
8 Wash and dry the paintwork and tiles with detergent and warm water.
9 Wash the floor with disinfectant and warm water.

Questions

1 **List the cleaning jobs in (a) the kitchen, (b) the living-room, and (c) the bathroom, which you would try to do every day.**
2 **Which rooms in the house is it especially important to keep thoroughly clean, and why?**
3 **Make a list of the extra jobs around the house which you would do when you were spring-cleaning.**
4 **Suggest some household jobs which any teenagers in the family could do regularly.**

Cleaning equipment and materials

It is a good idea to keep most of the items you use for cleaning together in one cupboard, away from cooking utensils or food. Always remember to keep polishes, bleaches and cleaners out of the reach of small children, as many of these everyday household items are poisonous if swallowed. Never transfer them into old lemonade bottles.

Having the right tools and cleaners makes it much easier to do a job well. You will need most of the following items for everyday cleaning:

Equipment
Hard broom (for outside)
Soft broom
Dustpan and brush
Upholstery brush
Vacuum cleaner (see page 98)
Attachments
Carpet sweeper
Mop, bucket
Dusters
Floorcloth
Cleaning rags
Chamois leather for windows

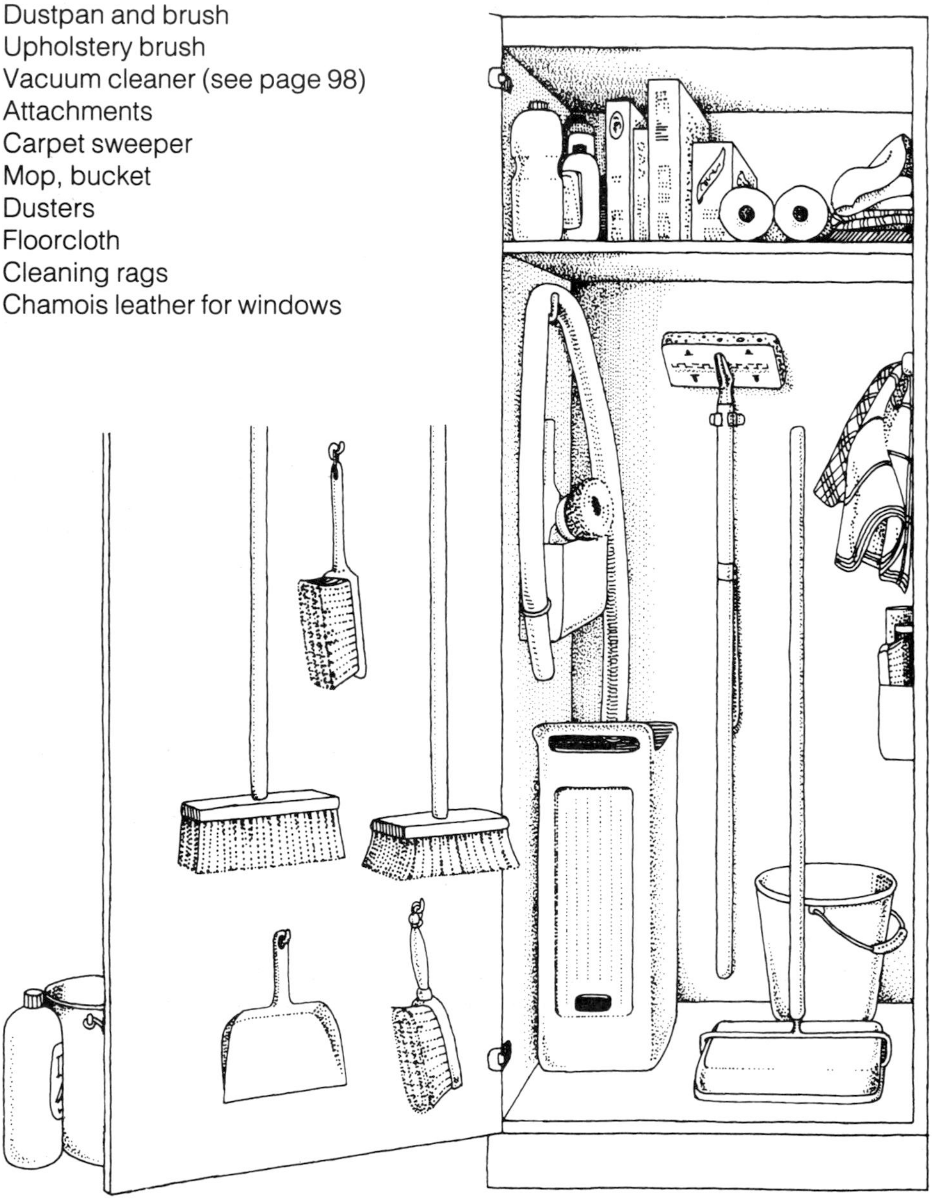

Materials
Polish for furniture and floors
Metal polishes – for silver, brass, copper
Cleaner for windows and mirrors
Liquid detergent (washing-up liquid)
Non-scratch cleaner for working surfaces, sink, cooker, etc.
Scouring powder
Soda for drains
Disinfectant for sinks, general cleaning
Bleach
Products for washing clothes (see page 130)

Comparing different products

There is such a variety of cleaning products available in the shops that it is useful to compare them to find out which suits you best. You can buy furniture polish, for example, as a spray, a wax or a liquid. You can use a spray, a liquid, or warm water and a wash-leather to clean the windows.

Look at different products made for the same purpose and compare:
1 The cost of the bottle, aerosol or packet, and the quantity it contains.
2 How long you would expect it to last.
3 Which involves most effort, or hard rubbing?
4 Which gives the best results?
5 Does it have a pleasant smell?
6 Can it harm or scratch surfaces?
7 Can you use it for different cleaning jobs?

Aerosols
Many household cleaners and toiletries are available as aerosol sprays. Although they are easy and convenient to use, it is thought that some of the chemicals used to propel the contents out of the can are damaging the ozone layer around the earth – that is, the part of the earth's atmosphere which protects us from any harmful effect of the sun's rays.

Questions
1 **How can you avoid the danger of a child being accidentally poisoned in the home?**
2 **Look at the list of cleaning equipment and materials. Write a list of the items you would consider necessary for your own home.**
3 **What points would you look for in buying**
   a furniture polish
   b a product for cleaning windows
   c a product for cleaning kitchen work surfaces?
4 **What are the advantages and disadvantages of using aerosol sprays?**

Vacuum cleaners

How vacuum cleaners work

A vacuum cleaner is an efficient way of cleaning as it collects dust and dirt and does not just move it from one place to another. A motor blows air out of the cleaner. This creates a vacuum. Air is sucked into the vacuum to replace the air blown out, and the dust and dirt are sucked in with the air. The dirt is collected either in a cloth bag which is later emptied, or in a disposable paper bag which can be thrown away and replaced. Although disposable bags are cleaner to use, the cost of buying them has to be considered. The bag should never be allowed to get more than half-full, or it will not work efficiently. For one unit of electricity you can do between two and four hours' cleaning.

Types of vacuum cleaner

Cylinder type
With this kind it is easier to get into awkward corners and under low furniture. It has to be put together when you want to use it and taken to pieces when you have finished with it, but this does not take long. This kind can be used for cleaning lino, vynolay or polished wooden floors and is quicker and better than sweeping them with a brush.

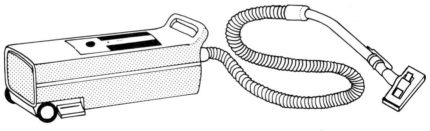

Upright type
This is quicker for large areas of carpet. It beats the carpet as it cleans it, which loosens the dirt and makes it easier to pick up. There is a brush underneath which picks up threads which would otherwise stick to the carpet. These threads should be removed from the brush when you finish cleaning. Usually the handle can be lowered to make it possible to reach under low furniture.

Attachments may be fitted to both types of cleaner, for dusting, for upholstery or curtains, or for cleaning down the sides of armchairs where it is hard to reach.

Carpet sweepers

These are useful for brushing over the carpet in between vacuuming. They pick up threads and crumbs very efficiently though they do not clean dust and dirt from down in the pile of the carpet.

When choosing a sweeper try to test it before you buy. Some models are much more efficient than others. Look for one whose handle stays upright and does not fall to the floor. A very small sweeper will have to be emptied frequently; a very lightweight one may spill fluff on to the floor.

Electric scrubber/polisher

This is invaluable if you have a lot of polished wood or lino floors. It will save you a lot of hard work. It has stiff brushes which rotate to scrub the floor and soft pads to attach beneath the brushes when you want to use it for polishing.

Shampooer
Some electric polishers can be used for shampooing carpets. They have a shampoo container and special shampooing brushes.

Dustette

A dustette is a very small, lightweight vacuum cleaner, which can easily be carried in the hand. It is useful for cleaning the stairs, or for cleaning inside a car.

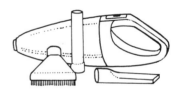

Questions
1 **What are the advantages and disadvantages of:**
   a a cylinder-type vacuum cleaner
   b an upright vacuum cleaner?
   Which kind would you prefer for your own home?
2 **List the different cleaning jobs which could be done with the attachments on a vacuum cleaner.**
3 **What points would you look out for when buying a carpet sweeper?**
4 **Why is an electric scrubber/shampooer/polisher useful? List the different brushes and pads which can be fitted to it.**
5 **List four cleaning jobs for which a dustette would be useful.**

Household pests

Woodworm

Woodworm in houses is mainly caused by the furniture beetle, a small brown insect about 3 mm long. The beetle attacks dry timber such as the floor, stairs or furniture in a house, and lays eggs which develop into the 'woodworm'. The worm bores into the wood, feeding on it, for about three years, then tunnels its way out to mate.

Look carefully for the signs – small round holes and sawdust nearby in house timber and old furniture. Liquids such as 'Rentokil' can be used to treat the wood and kill the beetle or worm, but where damage is extensive the infested wood may have to be cut out, burned and replaced with new treated timber.

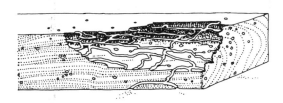

Rodents

Rats and mice are a serious health hazard. They eat and spoil food, contaminating it with their droppings. They can carry fleas and spread disease and dirt.

Food must always be stored in closed containers or cupboards where it cannot attract rodents. Dustbins should have firmly fitting lids.

If you see any signs of rats or mice, such as droppings or food packets that have been gnawed, you should immediately get in touch with the Rodent Officer from your local council. He will help you get rid of the infestation with suitable poisons or traps.

Fleas

Fleas can be brought into the house by cats and dogs. They lay eggs in carpets, furniture and house dust. Sprays and powders can be bought to treat them, and the local council will usually give help and advice on the best way to get rid of them.

Flies

Flies can carry many serious diseases. They feed and lay eggs on food and decaying rubbish, moving from one to the other and spreading bacteria from their bodies. When eating they excrete a saliva which is mixed with the food, then sucked back into their mouths.

All food must be kept covered to discourage flies. Rubbish bins should be kept clean and firmly closed.

Flies can be killed by swatting, or by using an aerosol spray in a closed room with food covered. Another product is available which hangs in the room giving off a vapour poisonous to flies. This lasts for several months. However, it is thought that the vapour could be harmful to humans as well as flies.

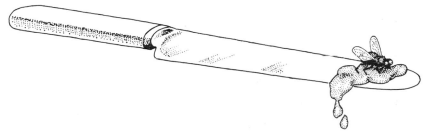

Cockroaches

Cockroaches live in dark, warm, places – near hot pipes, ovens or boilers. They come out at night to look for food, spreading bacteria from their sticky bodies and infecting food with their droppings.

Food should be stored away from warm places, but if any infestation occurs, all dark corners should be thoroughly cleaned out and special powder laid on the floor near skirtings and drains.

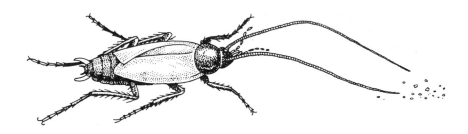

Questions

1 **List some hygiene rules every householder should follow to help prevent the infestation of any pests in the home.**
2 **What steps would you take to get rid of the following from an old house:**
   a rats and mice
   b fleas
   c cockroaches?
3 **What would you consider to be the safest way of killing flies in your kitchen?**

Further work on chapter 4

1   Choose a cleaning product commonly used in the home, e.g. furniture polish, window cleaner, or bath cleaner. Compare the products for this job that are available in the shops and select the one you would use yourself.

2   If you were married, with no children, and both partners had a full-time job, suggest how the routine housework could be divided fairly between you.

3   You have the opportunity to turn your bedroom into a bed-sitting room where your friends can visit you. Keeping within reasonable price limits, describe how you would like to decorate and furnish the room.

4   Carry out a study of the different methods of treating or curtaining windows, including plain curtains.

5   You have a small child who is ready to move from a cot to a single bed. You are deciding whether to choose blankets or a continental quilt and are comparing the two to help you decide which you would buy.

Sources of further information

Magazines, such as *Good Housekeeping, Which?, Family Circle*, and others.

The Good Housekeeping Institute, (address on page 124) has many different leaflets.

Rentokil Advice Centre, Felcourt, East Grinstead, West Sussex, has free leaflets and wallcharts, books, videos, etc. on household pests (including rodents and insects) and other subjects.

You can get ideas on decorating and effective colour schemes from displays in furniture and department stores, and shops like Next, Laura Ashley, and Habitat, as well as from magazines.

Books
Libraries often have books with large colour photographs which will give you ideas on room furnishings and decoration (often on the 'large sized books' shelf).

The Good Housekeeping Book of the Home, Marks and Spencer PLC.

Superwoman by Shirley Conran.

Chapter 5

The kitchen

Kitchen planning

The more efficiently a kitchen is planned and laid out, the less energy the person working there has to waste walking from one part to another.

Most work in the kitchen involves food and is carried out in this order: storage → preparation → washing → cooking → serving.

The equipment used for this work is as follows: cupboard or refrigerator → work surface → sink → cooker → work surface.

This equipment should be placed as close as possible to cut down unnecessary walking from one item to another.

It is best to place the three main areas – sink, cooker and storage – at the three points of a triangle, not more than 7 metres apart, and linked by work surfaces. The sink and cooker should each have a work surface on both sides. Storage of food and utensils in everyday use is best provided by wall cupboards above the work surface and a refrigerator below.

This could give either of these two basic layouts which are both convenient and energy saving.

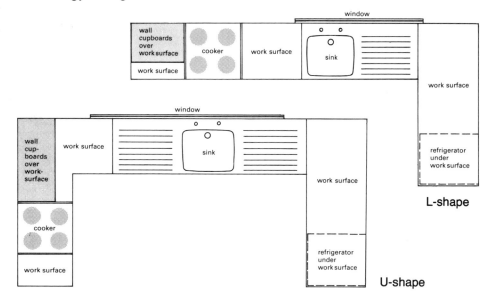

Once the position of these items of equipment has been settled, other items such as a washing machine, breakfast bar or table and chairs can be fitted in.

Work surfaces should be made of hard, easily-cleaned, heat- and stain-resistant material. Plastic laminates such as Formica and Melamine are ideal. You should clean them by washing them with hot water and liquid detergent, and remove marks with a non-scratch cleaner.

Floors should be easy to clean, hard-wearing, attractive, and resistant to heat, grease and water. They should not be slippery, but warm, comfortable and not too noisy to walk on. Good quality vinyl is a good choice.

Other suitable coverings are washable kitchen carpet or carpet tiles, both of which are easy to vacuum clean and can be scrubbed if necessary. They are also warm and soft to walk on.

Walls must be easy to clean as they have to withstand a lot of steam and grease. A splash-back made of ceramic tiles behind the sink and cooker is useful. Suitable wall coverings are gloss or emulsion paint, washable or vinyl wallpapers, tiles, or wood panels treated with a seal.

Curtains should be easy to wash and iron. If the window is near the cooker, avoid curtains which could blow on to the flame and catch fire. Venetian or roller blinds are suitable as long as they are washable.

Lighting in a kitchen should be good. Daylight is best whenever possible. Fluorescent strip lighting is ideal as it casts no shadows. Though a little more expensive to install than ordinary lighting it costs less to run.

Ventilation is important in a kitchen as it removes steam and grease which will otherwise settle on surfaces and make them difficult to keep clean. You can keep a window open when cooking, or use a cooker hood or extractor fan (see page 69).

Sinks Modern kitchen sinks come in a wide range of shapes and sizes. You can have one or two bowls, round or rectangular, one of which may be smaller, for rinsing or for preparing vegetables. They may come with a chopping board to fit over the draining board to give an extra work surface, or with fitted wire crockery baskets.

Materials used for sinks

1   Modified polycarbonate is the newest material. These sinks are attractive to look at and are available in several colours. They are hygienic, very resistant to heat, stains, and chemicals and energy-saving because they retain the heat of the hot water used in them. They are very quiet in use and greatly reduce the loud clattering of cutlery and dishes.
2   Stainless steel is hardwearing, easy to clean, but expensive and noisy.
3   Vitreous enamel is less expensive and available in a choice of colours. It wears well if you avoid clashing it with metal pans or utensils.
4   Fireclay sinks are fairly hard-wearing, but not installed in new houses now except as an extra sink for laundry. The join between the sink and wooden draining-board could harbour dirt and bacteria. The modern one-piece sink and draining-board is more hygienic and easier to clean.
5   Plastic or fibre-glass sinks are not hard-wearing enough for everyday use, but are adequate for occasional use – in a caravan, for example.

Questions

1   **Why is it important to have a well-planned kitchen?**
2   **What is the usual order of handling food when preparing a meal?**
3   **What are the main work areas involved in preparing a meal?**
4   **What three areas in the kitchen should be at the three points of an imaginary triangle?**
5   **Draw a diagram of a well-planned kitchen which has room for meals to be eaten.**
6   **What are the main points to consider when choosing each of the following for a kitchen: work surfaces, floor-covering, wall-coverings, curtains, lighting and sink unit?**

Fitted kitchens and cookers

Fitted kitchens

Cookers are often built-in nowadays as part of a fitted kitchen. The oven and hotplate are built into the workbenches giving an attractive streamlined effect which is also very easy to keep clean. There are no awkward places behind the cooker which are difficult to reach. Not only the cooker but refrigerators, freezers, dishwashers, cooker hoods, and microwave ovens can be built in too. These are designed to take a decor panel at the front which exactly matches the cupboard fronts, and the sink is fitted into the work surface.

These fitted kitchens look neat and are easy to keep clean, but they do have some disadvantages. They are expensive to install, especially as you would normally have to buy and fit everything (cooker, benches, cupboards, fridge, freezer, dishwasher, sink) at the same time to get a perfect match. You could not take any of the items with you if you moved house. You would also have to consider, if you were thinking of moving into a house with a fitted kitchen, that the fridge, cooker, and so on have all been used by someone else and so may not necessarily be as clean as you would like.

Cookers

There have been many developments in gas and electric cookers in recent years. These have improved their appearance, efficiency, economy with fuel, safety, and ease of cleaning.

Some of the new features available on both gas and electric cookers include:

Colour Cookers can be bought not only in white but in other colours (usually fairly neutral shades of brown) to match the kitchen.

Hobs, ovens and grills These can be bought completely separately if required. A hob can be set into the work surface so that it forms part of the bench. Ovens can either be built under a work surface (under the hob if you like, but not necessarily) or into another part of the kitchen. This means that the oven can be above waist level, making it easier to reach inside without having to bend down. You may find it useful to have storage space above or below the oven.

Slide-in cookers are made with the traditional oven, hob, and grill in one piece. They are made to fit neatly into a gap in the work benches to give a very snug fit and streamlined appearance. As there is hardly any gap at the side, cleaning is made easier. They are not built in so you can take them with you if you decide to move house.

A lid can be fitted on a cooker to cover the hob when it is not in use. When down over the hob the lid is completely level with the work bench, giving extra working space. Some lids can even be fitted with a decor panel to match the work top. When the lid is raised it makes an easily cleaned splash back. Some can be fitted with a hob light.

Thermostatic controls can form part of electric or gas hotplate rings. You set the temperature you want and the temperature of the saucepan is controlled so that it is less likely to boil over.

Grills whether gas or electric, are now often contained neatly within an oven. They may be in a second, smaller oven or in the main oven. It is more convenient if it is in a separate oven as otherwise you cannot use the oven and grill at the same time. Grilling inside the oven can be messy but this need not be a problem if the oven has a self-clean lining. Some grills have an attachment for spit roasting.

Self clean oven linings These provide a great saving of time and effort. Any fat which splashes during cooking is absorbed into the surface of the lining and slowly oxidized by the air, helped by the heat of the oven during cooking. This action continues all the time the oven is on and works best in a hot oven. The linings work most satisfactorily if a pattern of low then high temperature cooking is followed. For example, if low temperature roasting causing splashing is followed by high temperature baking, then cleaning is carried out effectively. Any bad spillage should be removed with a damp cloth or a weak solution of washing-up liquid. Never use any other cleaner and always follow the manufacturer's instructions.

Cleaning the hotplate is easy on a modern cooker. Electric ceramic hobs are extremely easy to clean (see page 108). Gas hotplates have sealed hobs and burners, and spillage bowls to catch any spillage. If pan supports are removable, they can be soaked and washed in the sink.

Automatic controls are available on many cookers. They incorporate a clock and minute minder. They will switch the oven on and off at any time you set. If you go out it can switch itself on, cook the meal for your return, and switch off. Some have sophisticated, electronic microchip controls providing fingertip control and a digital clock. Gas cookers require a nearby electric point to operate automatic controls.

Economy features may include a grill (either gas or electric) where you turn only part of it on, and electric rings where you turn only the centre part on for a small pan. If you have a double oven you need only switch on the smaller oven for most of your cooking. These are more often found in electric cookers, but are available too in some gas models. With both, the grill is in the smaller oven.

Microwave cookers can be built into the kitchen, sometimes as part of a fitted oven and grill unit. There is more information about microwave cookers on page 110.

Questions

1 **Describe the points for and against having a fully fitted kitchen.**
2 **Which kitchen appliances can be bought which will take a 'decor panel' to match cupboard fronts?**
3 **Where would you expect to find the grill in a slide-in cooker, or a built-in cooker with a single oven?**
4 **How would you care for a self-clean oven lining?**
5 **Would you expect a gas hob or an electric one to be easier to clean? Explain your answer.**
6 **What features might you find in modern gas and electric cookers to make them cheaper to run?**

Electric and gas cookers

Electric cookers

Electric cookers are often cleaner in use than gas and easier to clean, but they are less easy to control quickly.

A ceramic hob has the rings fitted inside one sheet of glass ceramic. The surface is smooth and easy to clean and is not readily scratched or stained. You have to use pans with a heavy base on these and other electric cookers.

The latest development to greatly improve the instant response and immediate control of heat is cooking by infra-red light, by *halo-heat*. Built into a ceramic surface are special tungsten halogen lamps. When you switch on, the reaction is immediate. 80% of the infra-red light (the heat) passes through the hob, into the pan and contents, and cooking begins immediately. When you turn the heat up or down the response is as immediate as on a gas flame. You may be able to see these hobs demonstrated at your electricity showroom.

Electric ovens have an even temperature. Most of them now have a fan to circulate the warm air. This causes the oven to heat quickly and is economical with fuel, as dishes can often be cooked at a lower temperature than traditionally. It also keeps the temperature of every shelf at the same level, rather than the oven being hotter at the top.

Slide-in cookers: electric (left) and gas (right)

Gas cookers

Gas cookers are generally more immediately controlled than electric cookers, although they are not quite as clean in use nor as easy to clean. However, the features of modern cookers described above have reduced the differences between the two, and now gas cookers have become easier to clean and electric cookers easier to control.

The temperature in a gas oven varies slightly. The setting on the control refers to the centre of the oven; the top will be a little hotter, the bottom cooler. This can be useful because dishes needing slightly different temperatures can be cooked at the same time.

Modern gas cookers have a *flame failure device* which cuts off the supply of gas if the flame should go out accidentally. They also have automatic or press button ignition, which does not need a pilot light and therefore saves gas.

Choosing a cooker

Gas or electric? This is a matter of personal choice. Many people choose what they have always been used to, but if you are buying a new one it is a good idea to try to look at both kinds with an open mind. Now that you can buy separate ovens and hotplates, the combination of gas hotplate for instant control and an electric oven for even heat is a possible choice.

General points to consider:

1 How many people you have to cook for every day and on special occasions.
2 The kind of cooking you do and how often.
3 How much you can afford to pay.
4 The amount of space you have in your kitchen.
5 How easy the cooker is to control and clean.
6 Does it have energy-saving features which will make it cheaper to run?
7 Is there a gas or electric point close to where you want to place the cooker? You can have the point moved, but this is an extra expense.
8 Not all houses have a mains gas supply but it is possible to buy full-sized cookers which work off a bottled supply of butane gas.
9 People who live in high-rise blocks may not be allowed to use gas cookers.
10 If the cooker is to be used by a disabled person, can you have special taps or switches fitted? (See page 29.)
11 Find out what *Which?* magazine has to say about the models you are thinking of buying (see page 162).

Questions

1 **What is probably the main advantage of an electric cooker over a gas cooker?**
2 **What is probably the main advantage of a gas cooker over an electric cooker?**
3 **Describe the way in which cooking by 'Halo-heat' improves the speed of response in an electric cooker hob.**
4 **Do you think it is an advantage to have a gas oven where the temperature is hotter at the top and cooler at the bottom? Explain your answer.**
5 **If you were choosing a new cooker for yourself, which kind would you choose? Explain the reasons for your choice.**

Microwave cookers

What are they?

A microwave cooker is a small oven which is simply plugged into any 13-amp socket and placed on a convenient work surface or table.

How does it work?

A magnetron inside the cooker produces electromagnetic rays, similar to radio waves. Food is made up of moist molecules and the electromagnetic rays cause these molecules to vibrate over two million times per second. This vibration generates heat within the food and cooks it.

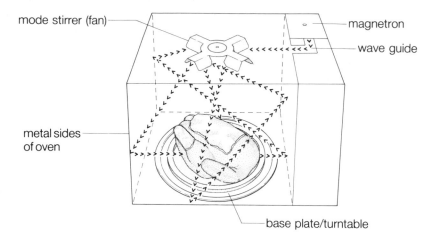

The advantages of microwave cooking

1   Food is cooked very quickly, in minutes and seconds rather than hours. Because of this you save money on fuel as well as saving time.
2   The cooker stays clean in use and is easy to keep clean.
3   Washing up takes less time after microwave cooking than after conventional cooking. You do not use saucepans and you may use the same dish to cook and serve the food. Food does not burn or stick to dishes.
4   A microwave cooker will defrost frozen food quickly and then cook it, so that the food (perhaps a casserole, loaf of bread, or chop) can be thawed and cooked in a fraction of the time it would take otherwise. For example, a bread roll taken from the freezer can be thawed and ready to eat in one minute.
5   Because food, especially vegetables, cooks quickly and in a small amount of water, it keeps its flavour and vitamin content.
6   A microwave oven will warm food fast, for example, a sausage roll will be heated through in one minute, a bowl of soup in two minutes.
7   If a meal is being cooked for the family and one person is expected to be late, then his or her portion may be put on a plate, covered with food-safe cling film, and heated up in a couple of minutes when the late-comer gets home.
8   The cooker is useful for a variety of odd jobs such as melting jelly cubes, softening butter from the fridge in seconds, cooking frozen vegetables in the bag in which they are bought, reheating drinks, making jam and marmalade, and raising yeast mixtures.

The disadvantages of microwave cooking

1 Microwave ovens are expensive to buy. Most households would want an ordinary gas or electric cooker as well, and a microwave (costing between £80 and £400) can cost as much as an ordinary cooker.
2 Space has to be found for it on a work surface or table in the kitchen or nearby. If space is limited, the oven can be placed on a strong, purpose-built shelf above the work surface.
3 Most microwave ovens do not make food brown or crisp. If you want meat to look acceptably brown you can either brown it under the grill or buy a special browning dish, which gives good results, but is an added expense. Cakes and puddings do not become golden brown, so recipes which include some dark ingredients such as cocoa, brown sugar, or ginger look the most appetizing.
4 A microwave is more useful for cooking small quantities than large quantities. When you cook large amounts of food you have to increase the cooking time so much, that often you may as well use a conventional oven. For example, although one baked potato cooks in just six minutes, six baked potatoes would take 60 minutes, so if you are cooking for several people, you do not necessarily save time. Neither can you always cook several things at once as you can in an ordinary oven.

How to choose a microwave oven

1 Go and look in the shops at the different models available and compare the cost and features of each.
2 You pay a higher price for models with more sophisticated features. By studying what is available you can decide whether or not it is worth paying extra for them. They may include:
a Touch controls linked to a microprocessor.
b A temperature probe to test whether meat is thoroughly cooked.
c Automatic timers to start cooking if you are out.
d Memory banks which store cooking programs for recipes you use regularly.
3 Choose a cooker whch is B.E.A.B. approved.
4 When you find a model you like, look it up in *Which*? magazine (at your library).

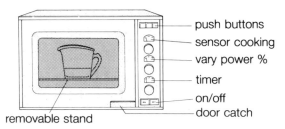

push buttons
sensor cooking
vary power %
timer
on/off
door catch
removable stand

Microwave ovens: manually operated (above) and electronically operated (below)

clock
on/off
touch controls
programs
door open
turntable (not visible)

Using the microwave

Cooking by microwave is quite different from conventional cooking, but if you follow your instruction booklet carefully you should soon find microwave cookery simple and convenient. Classes in microwave cookery may be available in your area. These can give you useful ideas and suitable recipes.

How to use

It is basically very simple to use. The most important control is the *timer*, set in minutes or seconds, because cooking is done by time and not temperature. It is easy to overcook food because it cooks so quickly. Cookers vary in wattage, so it is important to follow the instructions for your particular model. The simpler models have two power settings – cook and defrost; more sophisticated models have variable power control, giving more or less microwave energy, in the same way as the dimmer on a light switch. Some models have a turntable to rotate the food so that it cooks evenly.

Suitable cooking utensils

Most dishes and containers are suitable, but metal containers must never be used. Do not use aluminium foil, foil containers, or any china with gold or silver painted decorations.

Suitable materials for dishes include china, pottery, glass, most plastics including boil-in-the-bags, food-safe cling film, and roasting bags. All of these are suitable because the microwaves can pass through them into the food. Metal reflects the microwaves away from the food and so it does not cook. Metal can also damage the cooker.

Microwave cooking dishes

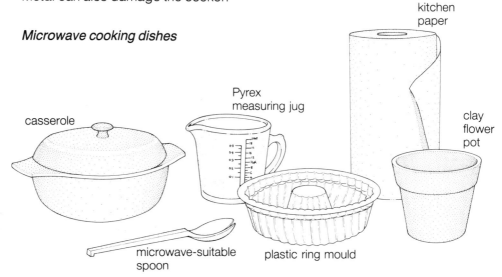

kitchen paper

Pyrex measuring jug

clay flower pot

casserole

microwave-suitable spoon

plastic ring mould

You can buy specially made bowls and dishes to use in the microwave where you would normally use a cake tin or baking tray. They are quite cheap to buy and look like a soft plastic material but they can be washed and re-used several times. Some kinds of microwave dishes can also be used in an ordinary gas or electric oven up to a certain temperature, and can be used in the freezer. These are useful because you could store a dish, e.g. macaroni cheese, in the freezer, defrost it in the microwave, and brown it off in the conventional oven, using the same dish all the time.

Browning dishes

Food does not become brown and crisp in the microwave, so some foods, such as meat, bacon, and sausages, can look pale and unappetizing. This can be overcome by using a browning dish (quite expensive to buy). The dish is pre-heated in the microwave oven and when the food is placed on it to cook, it becomes golden brown. Some more expensive models can be bought which have a built-in browning device similar to a grill.

How to keep it clean

The microwave oven stays much cleaner in use than a conventional oven, but in general:

1 Wipe any spillages with a damp cloth, but never use any abrasive cleaner.
2 Never use a knife or sharp utensil to scrape off hardened food.
3 Clean the outside of the cooker with a damp cloth, then polish with a dry cloth.

Repairs

Only a trained microwave engineer should attempt any repairs.

Questions
1 **How can a microwave oven be used to save fuel when cooking?**
2 **How could a microwave oven be useful to a single person out at work all day?**
3 **Describe three ways in which a family could find a microwave oven useful.**
4 **Describe two ways in which you could overcome the problem of the microwave cooker not browning food.**
5 **What sort of dishes (a) are safe to use (b) should never be used in the microwave oven?**
6 **What features could you expect to find on the most expensive models?**

Refrigerators and freezers

Refrigerators

Refrigerators are ideal for storing food. They are useful because:

1 They provide a cold, airtight compartment to keep food fresh and clean. The bacteria which make food go bad are not very active at this low temperature, which is usually below 7°C.
2 You can go shopping much less often as you do not have to buy fresh food daily but can store it.
3 Left-over food can be kept fresh, so there is less waste.
4 You can keep a ready supply of frozen food in the special storage compartment; as a stand-by for visitors, for when you do not have time to prepare a meal or for when you run out of food.
5 Some foods, such as cold puddings, milk, or fruit juice taste much nicer when served really cold.

How a refrigerator works

Refrigerators work on the principle that when liquids evaporate and turn to vapour (gas), they absorb heat to do this.

If you spill nail varnish remover or petrol on your hand it will absorb warmth from your skin to evaporate, making your hand feel cold.

A special liquid in the frozen food compartment evaporates, taking heat from the food in the fridge to do this. In this way, the food becomes cold. As the vapour cools it turns back to a liquid and again absorbs heat from the fridge. This cycle goes on continuously, keeping the food constantly cold.

How to use a refrigerator

1   Store food in the most suitable position. The part nearest the frozen food compartment is coldest, the door is the least cold.
2   Cover food before placing in the fridge, to prevent it from drying out.
3   Never put hot food into a fridge, as it will raise the temperature.
4   Do not open the door unnecessarily.
5   Arrange food on the shelves so that cold air can circulate freely.
6   When going on holiday empty the fridge, switch it off and open the door.
7   Never refrigerate bananas (they go black), root vegetables or apples.
8   Wrap strong-smelling foods well, or other foods may absorb their smell.

How to look after your refrigerator

Defrost it regularly, as soon as the ice on the freezing compartment is as thick as a pencil. Defrosting may be:

Fully automatic – it may switch off, defrost and switch back on whenever necessary, completely automatically.

Semi-automatic – a push-button is pressed when you wish to defrost. When defrosting is complete it switches itself on again.

Manual – you switch off, remove the food and wrap any frozen food in several layers of newspaper to keep it cool. Defrosting can be speeded up by placing a bowl of hot water in the freezing compartment. When all the ice has melted into the drip tray, this can be emptied and replaced. Wipe out the fridge and dry it, replace the food and switch on.

Cleaning Wash the inside of the refrigerator with a solution of one tablespoon of bicarbonate of soda to one pint of warm water. Do not use detergent as the smell may linger and affect the food. The outside can be washed with hot, soapy water and dried with a soft cloth. A little furniture cream should be used occasionally on the outside, to keep it in good condition.

How to choose a refrigerator

1   Choose one large enough to suit your family, or a little larger.
2   Make sure it will fit into the space available.
3   Consider the way in which it has to be defrosted.
4   Some refrigerators are combined with a separate small freezer (page 96).
5   Frozen food compartments have star markings which are a guide to their temperature and so to the length of time ready-frozen foods can be safely stored in them.

    ❄ The temperature is about −6°C.
    Food can be stored up to one week.
    ❄❄ The temperature is about −12°C.
    Food can be stored up to one month.
    ❄❄❄ The temperature is about −18°C.
    Food can be stored up to three months.

These frozen food compartments are for the storage of ready-frozen foods, they are not for freezing fresh foods. They are not cold enough to do this safely unless they have this extra star marking: ❄❄❄❄

Freezers

A freezer is designed to freeze fresh food and keep it at or below −18°C for long periods without spoilage.

Freezers have the following advantages:
1   You can have a good store of food always available, particularly if you live a long way from the shops.
2   If you have a large garden you can freeze your own fruit and vegetables for use later in the year.
3   You can buy fruit and vegetables when they are in season and at their best and cheapest.
4   You can 'batch-bake', preparing several dishes at one baking session and freezing those you do not need straight away.
5   Ready-frozen foods can be bought in bulk from supermarkets or 'freezer centres' at lower prices than normal.
6   Freezers are useful when cooking for a party as dishes can be prepared in advance, saving a last minute rush.

These disadvantages must also be considered:
1   The cost of buying and running the freezer. It will use about 1½–2 units of electricity for each cubic foot of space per week (1 unit per 1.5 litres).
2   The cost and time involved in preparing and packaging foods.
3   The possibility of food spoilage during a power cut, or the cost of insurance against this.
4   The cost of servicing or repair.
5   The space the freezer will occupy.

Types of freezer

Chest type Top-opening lid, a little cheaper to buy and run.

Upright type Front-opening door, easy to pack and unpack and to check food stocks. Uses less floor space.

Fridge/freezer Combines an upright freezer with a refrigerator in one cabinet. Useful where space is limited.

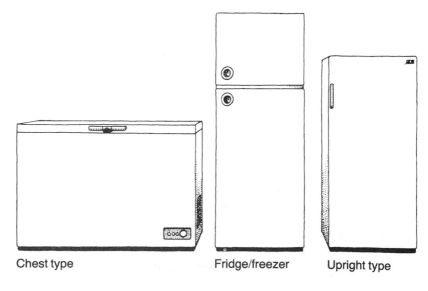

Chest type   Fridge/freezer   Upright type

Some rules for freezing food

1 Only freeze food which is in perfect condition.
2 Never re-freeze food once it has thawed. Bacteria increase rapidly in food which has previously been frozen.
3 All meat and poultry must be <u>completely</u> thawed before cooking.
4 Foods which freeze well: pastry, bread, cakes, meat, soups, stews and vegetables.
5 Some foods do not freeze well. These include salad vegetables, milk, eggs in shells, large fruits unless cooked (e.g. stewed apple).
6 Foods must be properly packaged and labelled.
7 Store food only for the recommended time.
8 Never put warm food in the freezer.
9 Open the freezer as little as possible.
10 Defrost the freezer regularly, according to the manufacturer's instructions.
11 When adding more than 1 kg of fresh food to the freezer, set the control to 'fast freeze'. This prevents the temperature from rising and causing food spoilage.

Packaging frozen foods

This must be carried out carefully, or foods may dry out and odours pass from one food to another.

Suitable materials: heavy-duty polythene bags, sheets of polythene for large, awkward shapes such as a turkey, plastic containers, foil and foil dishes. Special freezer tape and wire twists are suitable for closing bags.

All food should be clearly marked with the date and contents. It is useful to keep a book recording what you put in and take out of the freezer so that you know exactly what you have in stock.

Questions

1 **List six advantages of having a refrigerator.**
2 **Describe briefly how a refrigerator works.**
3 **Draw a diagram showing where in the fridge you would store: eggs, lard, fish-cakes, uncooked meat, a packet of frozen peas.**
4 **How should you cover the following before putting them into a fridge? (a) some Cheddar cheese, (b) a joint of meat, (c) some herrings, (d) slices of corned beef.**
5 **How often should you defrost a fridge? Describe how you would defrost it manually and thoroughly clean it.**
6 **Draw the four different star symbols found in refrigerators. Say what each means.**
7 **What do you consider would be the four main advantages to you of having a freezer?**
8 **List six costs involved in having a freezer.**
9 **What are the three main types of freezer? Give some points for and against each one.**
10 **Give the general rules you should follow when freezing food.**
11 **Name eight foods which it would be useful to have in store in your freezer. How would you pack and label each one?**

Dishwashers

Hundreds of hours are spent yearly, in every household, washing up after meals. A dishwasher can do this job for you, efficiently and hygienically. It is particularly useful in a large family or for a household which has a lot of visitors.

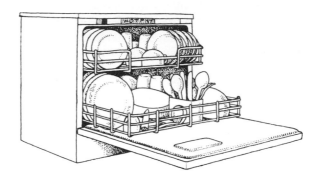

Sizes

There are different types and sizes available to suit the needs of most families. You can have one built into a fitted kitchen, or placed on top of a work-bench, or you can have a free-standing model. The size is measured by the number of place settings it will hold, usually between four and twelve.

Plumbing

Dishwashers can often be plumbed directly into the hot or cold water supply and as the cycle may take any time between about 20 and 90 minutes it is an advantage to have this done, so that the taps at the sink are free for normal use.

Hygiene

The dishwasher is often used only once a day. Dirty plates and utensils are stacked inside until it is full, then the day's washing-up is done all at once. The standard of hygiene is high, as a special detergent is used and the water is hotter than you could use at the sink. Because of this, however, hand-painted china, very fine glass, and cutlery with glued-on handles should not be placed in the machine. Most everyday articles are quite safe.

How it works

The dishwasher works by forcing a spray or jet of water around the dishes inside the machine. The pressure behind the water may be adjustable according to whether very dirty pans or fairly clean plates are being washed.
    As the normal washing-up after a meal includes china, glasses, cutlery and saucepans you want a machine which will give good overall results when loaded with a variety of different items.

Disadvantages

Although a dishwasher can be useful and labour-saving it does have disadvantages which should be considered if you are thinking of buying one.

1 The high cost which tends to make us think of dishwashers as a luxury rather than a necessity.
2 The cost of servicing and repair, to keep the dishwasher in good working order.
3 The cost of the special detergent and rinsing solution which are recommended for the best results.
4 The cost of having the machine plumbed in or else the inconvenience of having the taps unavailable for about an hour while the machine completes its cycle.
5 The time involved in rinsing all food scraps off plates or saucepans before they can be loaded.
6 The time and effort involved in loading the machine; unless there is a great deal of washing-up to be done it may be simpler and quicker to do it by hand in a bowl at the sink.
7 If you planned to run the machine only once a day, you might need to buy extra crockery and cutlery to last the day.
8 A dishwasher will use about one unit of electricity to wash the dinner dishes for a family of four.

To help you choose

When you are choosing any expensive household appliance it is important to find out as much as you can about the different kinds available. You can do this by:

a looking for information in the magazine 'Which?' (see page 162).
b asking for advice from your local Consumer Advice Centre.
c talking to friends who have one.
d studying the manufacturers' leaflets and instruction booklets.

Questions

1 **Name two kinds of household where a dishwasher might be very useful.**
2 **Describe a family who would probably find it simpler and easier to do their washing-up by hand.**
3 **Why is it best to have a dishwasher plumbed in?**
4 **What are the disadvantages of having a dishwasher?**
5 **List the different ways of finding information about different models, to help you choose between them.**
6 **Name three kinds of shops where you could go to look at different dishwashers.**
7 **List these household appliances in the order in which you would save up to buy them, if you had a limited amount of money to set up home: vacuum cleaner, cooker, dishwasher, waste disposal unit, washing machine, electric food-mixer, refrigerator, split-level cooker.**

Small kitchen equipment

The pressure cooker

The pressure cooker works on the principle that when the pressure inside the pan is increased by preventing the escape of steam, a higher temperature is produced which cooks food in a shorter time.

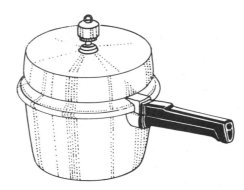

Advantages of having a pressure cooker

1   *Speed* Food can be cooked very quickly, in one-quarter to one-third of the usual cooking time. For example, a stew which would normally take two hours can be cooked in about twenty-five minutes, and potatoes can be cooked in six minutes.

2   *Fuel* can be saved, as food takes less time to cook, and as several foods can be cooked in the pan at the same time – for example, meat, potatoes and vegetables.

3   *The nutritive value* of food is high. Vegetables are cooked quickly and in steam rather than water, so there is a smaller loss of vitamins into the water.

4   *Cheaper, tougher cuts of meat,* which would otherwise take a long time to cook, can be pressure-cooked quickly and easily until tender.

5   *Different uses.* The cooker can be used for bottling fruit and vegetables to preserve them, for sterilizing baby's bottles, for making jam and marmalade, and for making baby foods.

How to use a pressure cooker

1   Study and follow the instruction book carefully, to gain confidence in controlling the cooker.

2   Do not overfill. The pressure cooker should be no more than half-full for liquids, two-thirds for solids.

3   Put the lid on, and place the cooker over high heat till a steady flow of steam comes through the vent. Add the weight which controls the amount of pressure in the cooker.

4   When a loud hiss is heard, start to time the food. Turn the heat down so that the cooker keeps up just a steady hiss.

5   Time food carefully, and do not overcook.

6   Cool either by leaving for about 5 to 10 minutes, or by running the cooker under cold water for a couple of minutes to reduce the pressure.

7   When the hissing stops, the control weight and lid may be removed.

How to care for a pressure cooker

As it is usually made of polished aluminium it should be washed in hot, soapy water, dried well and stored with the lid off. Check that the rubber gasket is clean and replace it when it lets steam escape. The cooker can be sent to the makers every five years or so for servicing.

The cost is fairly high, but the pan is strong and well made and should last for many years. Look around and compare prices before you buy.

Saucepans

Consider the following points when choosing from the wide variety available:

1 Heavier pans will spread heat more evenly and keep their shape better.
2 The pan should not be too heavy to lift easily.
3 Handles should be heat-resistant and firmly fixed.
4 Lids should fit well.
5 All pans used on electric cookers should have a heavy base.

Metals used to make saucepans

Aluminium. Probably the most widely used. It is available in different thicknesses. Fairly thick aluminium pans are strong, long-lasting, easy to clean and reasonably priced. They should give good service for many years.

Vitreous enamel on steel. Look for this sign as a guide to quality. These pans are often chosen for their very attractive patterns and colours, which make them a good choice for oven-to-table ware. They need more care in use than aluminium pans as the enamel may become scratched or discoloured. Never use metal utensils or scouring powder on them.

registered trade marks
of the Vitreous Enamel
Development Council Ltd

Enamel pans are cheap, but lightweight and easily chipped. They may be satisfactory for foods such as vegetables which do not easily stick.

Stainless Steel is very expensive, but hard and strong. Pans tend to be thin because of the cost, so they often have a heavy base of aluminium or copper added, to spread heat evenly and prevent sticking. Wash them in hot, soapy water, and dry them straight away to prevent them becoming marked.

Non-stick finish is a coating of P.F.T.E., a plastic which may be applied to pans, baking tins and oven linings, to make them much easier to wash. If it is of good quality it should last quite well provided that you avoid scratching it. Never use metal utensils or metal pan cleaners in it, and never use scouring powder. A wash with hot, soapy water should be all that is needed. When used in baking tins it helps cakes to be more easily removed from the tin, though tins should still be lightly greased.

Small electrical appliances

Mixers

Mixers vary in power from a full-sized mixer with a large bowl and stand to smaller hand-mixers. They do not use much electricity, so they are quite cheap to run – one unit is enough for over sixty cakes to be mixed.

Mixers can be used for a variety of jobs: creaming cake mixtures, rubbing fat into flour, whipping cream or egg whites. Some larger models have a dough hook for kneading dough.

The mixer should be kept ready for use on a work bench. If it is put away in a cupboard you are less likely to use it often. Covers can be bought or made to keep it free from dust. Hand-mixers usually have a bracket for fixing them to the wall in a convenient place.

Attachments may be bought for some mixers to do a variety of jobs – slicing and shredding vegetables, extracting juice, grinding coffee beans, peeling vegetables, mincing meat. Provided they are strongly made and easy to attach and clean, attachments can be quick and labour-saving.

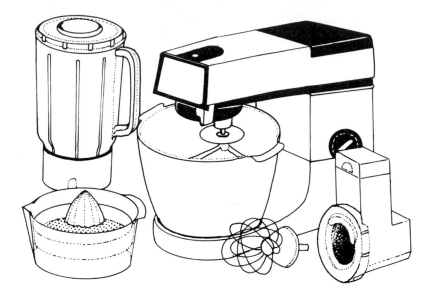

Blenders

Blenders (or liquidizers) are very useful. They sometimes come as attachments to mixers or they may be bought separately. They are ideal for blending soups, making a puree of fruit or vegetables, chopping nuts, making crumbs from bread, biscuits or cakes and making baby foods.

They are inexpensive to run – one unit of electricity would blend about 500 pints of soup.

The blender should be used carefully, following the manufacturer's instructions. It should not normally be run for long periods as the motor may overheat. The best way to clean the goblet is to rinse off most of the food particles under the tap, half fill with warm water, add a drop of detergent and put the lid on. Switch on for a few seconds, rinse and dry. Unplug the motor and wipe with a damp cloth.

Never put the motor unit into the water.

Toasters

It is more economical to use a toaster than to heat a grill just to make toast. One unit of electricity will toast about 70 slices of bread. Automatic 'pop-up' toasters will prevent toast burning. Some can toast up to four slices, lightly or well done.

You should never poke with a metal knife to loosen toast while the toaster is still plugged in, as this could give you an electric shock.

Slow cooker

This is a large, well-insulated pan which can be plugged in, switched on and left to cook slowly all day. You could start a stew cooking in the morning, go out, and return to a hot, well-cooked meal. The cooker is well sealed to keep in moisture and flavour and is ideal for the long, slow cooking of inexpensive, tougher cuts of meat. It is quite economical, using only about the same amount of electricity as a light bulb.

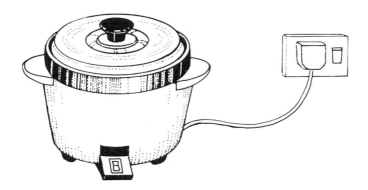

Food processors

Food processors will process food in a variety of different ways without your having to buy any extra accessories. They will mix, cream fat and sugar, rub fat into flour, blend, mince, chop, slice, shred and knead. They perform all these operations very quickly, faster than a food mixer.

However, as they are not able to take large quantities at one time, they are not necessarily more useful than a mixer. Whether they are a better buy for you than a mixer depends upon the kind of food preparation you do most. If you do a lot of slicing or shredding of vegetables, or make a lot of marmalade or chutney, or mince your own meat, then they could save you a lot of time. But if you want a mixer more for making cakes and kneading dough for bread, or if you want to bake large quantities in bulk, perhaps for a freezer, then an electric mixer, maybe with a blender and a slicer/shredder, would be a more useful buy for you.

You should always look for the B.E.A.B. (British Electrotechnical Approvals Board) sign on any electrical appliance you want to buy. (See page 32.)

Questions

1 **What are the advantages of using a pressure cooker?**
2 **What important points should you look for when choosing pans?**
3 **Name three metals used to make saucepans, giving the points for and against each.**
4 **How should you look after pans, baking tins or oven-linings with a non-stick finish?**
5 **Name the three small electrical appliances you would most like in your kitchen. How would each be useful and how would you use and care for them?**

Further work on chapter 5

1   Write a short report on the cooker you use most, whether at home or at school, assessing its good and bad features.

2   You want to choose a microwave cooker, as reasonably priced as possible. You live by yourself so usually cook for one only. How would you select the cooker?

3   You always seem to be walking from one end of the kitchen to the other when you are cooking. How could you rearrange the storage of different items so that you walk about as little as possible?

4   Your mother wants to buy a fridge-freezer and you are going to help choose one that is suitable. How would you do this?

5   You are living in your own flat on a very tight budget. Would you use all the disposable paper, polythene, and foil products available for kitchen use?

Sources of further information

British Gas Education Service (address on page 52) has leaflets, films and videos on cookers, kitchen planning, and other subjects. A catalogue of their material is available.

Gas and electricity showrooms and stores have leaflets describing most of their goods.

Which? magazine describes and compares many kitchen goods and appliances.

Good Housekeeping Institute, National Magazine House, 72 Broadwick St., London W1V 6BP produces booklets and leaflets on many topics. Send s.a.e. for full list.

Lakeland Plastics, Alexandra Buildings, Windermere, Cumbria have leaflets and videos on home freezing, microwave cooking, ovenware, and accessories.

Film
EFVA (address on page 52): 'Cookers – getting the best out of them'.

Book
Microwave Cookery by Cecilia Norman, Oxford University Press.

Chapter 6

The family washing

Ways to do your washing

There are many different ways of coping with the family wash, from a bowl of hot, soapy water at the sink to an automatic electronic machine. The equipment you choose will probably depend on:

a the money you have available

b the size of your family

c the time you can spend doing the washing.

Here are some of the ways you can get your washing done.

The launderette

Advantages

1 You do not have the cost of buying a machine.
2 They are quite cheap to use compared to the cost of buying, running and servicing your own.
3 Clothes can be washed and completely dried.
4 They are useful for large items such as blankets, even if you have a machine at home.
5 They are useful for drying clothes washed at home in wet weather, although some launderettes will not allow you to do this.

Disadvantages

1 Getting to the launderette and waiting around for washing to be done is time-consuming. Sometimes you can leave your washing in the care of an attendant and collect it later.
2 The results are not always very good, especially if you put different kinds of materials in the same wash-load to save expense.

The laundry

The laundry will collect and deliver to your home. You parcel up the items to be washed, writing each item on a list. A laundry van calls once a week to collect them, returning them a week later, washed and ironed. There is a set charge for each article, depending on its size.

Advantages

1   There is no work involved for you. Your laundry is returned clean and well ironed.
2   If you are likely to be out when the van calls, you can take the laundry to a shop and collect it at a time which suits you.

Disadvantages

As each item is charged separately, it would be very expensive to do all the washing for a family this way; it could be useful, though, for items like sheets, towels and pillowcases, while clothes could be hand-washed at home, particularly if there are only one or two people.

Washing by hand

This is hard work if there are more than a few small articles to be washed. It can be difficult to keep clothes a good colour, especially if they need very hot water. Hand washing is often best for delicate garments or fabrics. Pre-soaking in biological or other detergent makes hand washing easier, as does the use of a spin-dryer.

Washing by machine

You should consider the following points when choosing a machine:

1   The size, according to the size of your family. Size is measured by the weight of dry clothes the machine will hold, for example three kilos.
2   Does the machine have a built-in water heater? You may need one if you do not have a good supply of hot water.
3   Look for the B.E.A.B. label as a sign of safety.
4   Does the machine need a low-lather detergent?
5   Will it have to be plumbed-in to the water supply?
6   Find out all you can about a particular model you are thinking of buying. Ask friends, see if it has been tested by 'Which?', ask for information from your Consumer Advice Centre.
7   What type of machine do you want: automatic, twin tub, or a single tub with a wringer?

Questions

1   **Give as many reasons as you can why many people use launderettes to do their washing.**
2   **What are the points for and against sending some or all of your weekly washing to the laundry?**
3   **Describe two households where using a laundry for some or all of the washing would be suitable.**
4   **Make a list of all the clothes you can think of which would be best washed by hand.**
5   **You are helping a friend to choose a new washing machine. What do you think are the four most important points which she should consider carefully before spending her money?**

Types of washing machine

Single tub with a wringer

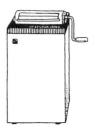

The wringer may be worked by hand or electricity. An electric wringer should have a safety device so that it can be quickly and easily knocked open if you get your fingers trapped.

The clothes may be washed either by the action of a paddle in the bottom of the tub (which is a slow, gentle action) or by a pulsator on the side of the tub. The action of the pulsator is quicker (perhaps four minutes instead of twelve to wash a load of clothes) but may be more likely to tangle the clothes. After the soapy water has been wrung out, the clothes are usually rinsed in the sink, then they are wrung again.

Twin tubs and automatics are becoming more popular than wringer machines. They are easier to use and extract more water from clothes than a wringer does.

Twin tub

This has one tub for washing and another for rinsing and spin-drying. As in the single-tub machine the clothes are washed by the action of either a pulsator or a paddle. Some twin tubs have a continuous rinsing action in the spin-drier. This means that clean water can be fed into the spinner at the same time as soapy water is pumped out of it until the rinsing water runs clear. Most twin tubs have a heater and timer so that clothes can be washed at the correct temperature and for the correct length of time.

Automatics

These have one tub for both washing and spinning. (Some more expensive models also tumble dry clothes in warm air in the same tub.) All you have to do with these machines is to put the clothes and detergent in, select the controls according to the water temperature, length of wash and length of spin required and switch on. The machine will wash, rinse and spin-dry without your help.

For economy, some models have a half-load facility. This means that if you have only a small load to wash, the machine uses much less hot water and washing powder, and saves electricity and money.

An automatic machine should be plumbed in to the water supply to leave the taps free while the machine is working. As these machines have more sophisticated controls than twin tubs they can be very expensive to repair if they go wrong. An automatic will be either a 'front loader' or a 'top loader'.

Front loader
1 Clothes are washed by a tumbling action in a revolving drum. This washing action is quite gentle, so that even delicate clothes can be washed safely.
2 Once it has started you can't open the door to add any more clothes.
3 A low-lather detergent must always be used – these are a little more expensive than others.
4 It takes up less kitchen space as it can be fitted under a work top.

Top loader
1 This washes the clothes by the action of a paddle.
2 Clothes can be added after the wash has started.
3 Any washing powder may be used.
4 It uses more kitchen space as it cannot have a work top built over it.

Front loader   Top loader

Which would you buy?

Twin tub
Same hot soapy water washes several loads.
More time and work involved.
Can spin clothes very dry.

Automatic
Hot water and detergent can be used for only one load.
No work involved, works automatically.
Does not usually spin quite so dry.
Should be plumbed in at extra cost.
May be more expensive to repair.

Prices of both types now tend to be similar.

Questions
1 **How does a machine with a wringer get clothes clean? How would you rinse them?**
2 **How are the clothes in a twin tub with a pulsator washed and rinsed?**
3 **Describe the washing action in a front-loading machine.**
4 **If you were buying an automatic machine would you choose a front loader or a top loader? Give all your reasons.**
5 **You are trying to decide whether to buy a twin tub or an automatic. Give the advantages and disadvantages of both kinds.**

Organizing your wash

Preparing the clothes before washing

1 Mend any tears and darn any holes as they are likely to get bigger in the wash.
2 Make sure all pockets are empty. A paper handkerchief, for example, could disintegrate and spread fluff over the rest of the washing.
3 Always close zips, otherwise they may not close smoothly afterwards.
4 Tie any apron strings or tapes so they won't get tangled.
5 Remove any stains before washing or ironing (see page 136).
6 Sort clothes according to the colour and the fabric they are made from, or according to the wash code labels (see page 132).

Which washing powder?

There are basically six different types of detergent for washing clothes. Each one is suitable for a particular purpose.

1 *Synthetic detergents,* e.g. Surf, Daz. These don't contain any soap. They are good for all general washing, by hand or machine (except front-loading automatics). They produce good lather even in hard water and are easy to rinse away.

2 *Soap powders* based on soap, e.g. Persil, Fairy Snow. They are made from natural animal or vegetable fats. They are good for all general washing by hand or machine, though in hard water areas they will not lather very well and may produce a scum.

3 *Biological (enzyme) detergents,* e.g. Ariel, Biological Daz. These are synthetic detergents which contain enzymes to break down and remove protein stains such as milk, blood or egg. They are very useful for soaking out stains before washing. They work best in water which is hand-hot but not above 60°C.

   Some fabrics – wool, silk and leather – should never be soaked. Garments with metal fasteners may not be suitable for soaking. Flame-resistant finishes should never be soaked but washed in hand-hot water.

   Clothes which are not colour-fast should not be soaked. To test for colour fastness, wash an inconspicuous part of the garment in a washing powder solution and iron it while damp between two pieces of white fabric. If any colour comes out or if you are in doubt, wash the article quickly and separately, in warm water (40°C).

4 *Low-lather detergents,* e.g. Bold, Persil Automatic. Specially made to be used in front-loading automatic machines, they produce only a small amount of foam, as too much would prevent the machine from working efficiently.

5 *Grease-solvent washing powders,* e.g. Drive. These are specially formulated to remove greasy marks and stains from clothes, for example, greasy marks from cotton/polyester pillowcases of shirt collars, or oily marks from dirty overalls. They are also useful for soaking out stains such as butter or lard.

6 *Light duty detergents* e.g. Dreft, Stergene. These are suitable for hand-washing lightly soiled clothes or for delicate fabrics and wool. They are easy to rinse away and leave clothes feeling soft.

7 *Cool water detergents* are available now. They wash well at low temperatures and so save money on the amount of electricity needed to heat the water.

Fabric Conditioners

These products – e.g. Comfort, Lenor – are not for cleaning clothes, but are added to the final rinsing water. They make clothes feel softer, add body to the fabric and reduce static electricity so that dirt is not attracted to the fabric. They give a soft, fluffy feel to wool, knitwear, towels and babies' nappies and leave clothes smelling nice.

Hypochlorite bleach

Bleach, e.g. Domestos, is useful for keeping white cotton and linen a good white colour or for removing stains from them. It is strong and poisonous if swallowed and should only be used exactly in accordance with the makers' instructions. Keep bleach away from children and store it carefully.

Starch

This gives a crisp, firm finish to cotton articles such as tablecloths, pillowcases, shirt collars and cuffs and it helps keep them clean for longer. It can be bought in powder or liquid form or as an aerosol spray which is convenient, quick and easy to use.

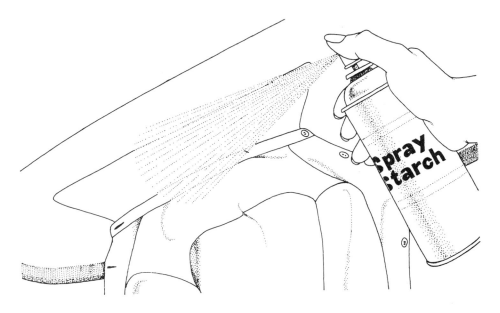

Questions

1 **How would you prepare and sort clothes before washing?**
2 **Describe the different types of washing powder in everyday use in the home, saying when each would be a suitable choice.**
3 **How do fabric conditioners improve your washing results? Name some garments to which they give a particularly good finish.**
4 **Which fabrics can be safely treated with hypochlorite bleach?**
5 **What are the advantages of starching cotton garments after washing?**

The H.L.C.C. labelling scheme

The Home Laundering Consultative Committee (H.L.C.C.) system of labelling clothes with washing instructions has been agreed between Britain and many other countries.

Nearly every garment you buy has a sewn-in label telling you exactly how to wash it to keep it in the best possible condition, according to the fabric it is made from. The labels give you the information listed below and should be followed carefully. A garment which is incorrectly washed just once can be completely spoiled and never restored to good condition.

1 The <u>temperature</u> of the water you should use. This may be:
100°C   Boiling
  95°C   Very hot though not quite boiling
  60°C   Hot – much too hot for the hands
  50°C   Hand-hot – just as hot as your hands can stand
  45°C   Warm – feels just warm to the touch
  30°C   Cool – feels rather cool to the hands

2 Whether the garment should have a long or short machine wash, be hand-washed or not washed at all.
The length of time the garment should be machine-washed varies according to how delicate or strong it is, and is described on the label as <u>maximum</u>, <u>medium</u> or <u>minimum</u>.

3 Whether you can spin, wring, drip-dry or tumble-dry.

4 Whether you can use chlorine bleach (e.g. Domestos).

May be treated with chlorine bleach

Do not use chlorine bleach

5 The correct temperature for ironing.

Hot (210°C)
for cotton, linen, rayon

Warm (160°C)
for polyester mixtures, wool

Cool (120°C)
for acrylic, nylon, polyester

Do not iron

6 If and how the garment can be <u>dry cleaned</u>. The letter in the circle tells the dry cleaner which fluid to use.

Do not dry clean

The wash code and how it is used

These labels are also found on most washing powder packets. If you know what fibre your garment is made from – and there is nearly always a label to tell you this sewn into it – you can follow the instructions and wash it correctly.

If you use an automatic, you just set your machine to the same washing process as the one on the label and the clothes will automatically have the correct programme.

If you use a twin tub or a single tub with wringer you follow the instructions under 'Machine wash'.

If you wash by hand, follow the instructions under 'Hand wash'.

All items with the same wash-code number can be safely washed together provided they are colour-fast.

White cotton and linen articles without special finishes

Cotton, linen or rayon articles without special finishes where colours are fast at 60°C

White nylon; white polyester/cotton mixtures

Coloured nylon; polyester; cotton and rayon articles with special finishes; acrylic/cotton mixtures; coloured polyester/cotton mixtures

Cotton, linen or rayon articles where colours are fast at 40°C, but not at 60°C

Acrylics; acetate and triacetate, including mixtures with wool; polyester/wool blends

Wool, including blankets, and wool mixtures with cotton or rayon; silk

Silk and printed acetate fabrics with colours not fast at 40°C

Cotton articles with special finishes capable of being boiled but requiring drip drying

Articles which must not be machine washed

Do not wash

Questions

1 **Why should you look for H.L.C.C. labels on the clothes you buy?**
2 **What are the water temperatures normally used for washing processes?**
3 **What do the terms <u>maximum</u>, <u>medium</u> and <u>minimum</u> mean when used on wash-care labels?**
4 **How would you wash and iron a woollen cardigan with this label?**

5 **How would you wash and iron a garment with this label?**

Drying and ironing

Drying

Spin-driers extract most of the water from the clothes although they don't actually dry them. A spin-drier may be part of a twin tub or bought separately. Automatic machines also spin-dry clothes at the end of the cycle.

After clothes have been spun-dried or wrung they have to be completely dried. This can be done in any of the following ways:

1   *Drying outside on a line* gives clothes a soft texture and a fresh smell, is cheap and keeps moisture out of the house. The action of sunlight on white cotton keeps it a good colour, though wool should not be dried in the sun.

2   *A tumble-drier* can be used. Clothes which have been spun or wrung are tumbled in a revolving drum in a flow of warm air. You set the temperature of the air and the length of time in the drier according to whether you want the clothes just dry enough to iron or completely dry, and according to the fabric they are made from. It is important to set these controls correctly if you want good results.

A tumble-drier is especially useful for giving a soft, fluffy finish to towels and nappies. Pure wool garments should never be tumble-dried. Always follow the recommendations of the manufacturer.

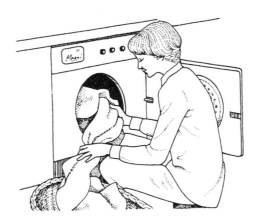

3   *Launderettes* have large-sized tumble-driers which you can sometimes use even if you wash the clothes at home.

4   *A pulley,* attached to the ceiling in a warm kitchen, is useful for drying and airing.

5   *A clothes-horse* will fold up when not in use. Some fit over the bath so that you can drip-dry clothes easily.

6   *Radiators* can be used, though clothes tend to become rather stiff and crumpled as they dry.

7   *Drying cupboards or cabinets* are less popular now for use in the home. Clothes are hung on rails or racks and warm air from a heater below dries them.

Whenever you have to dry washing indoors, by whatever method, make sure that the room is well ventilated to stop the air and walls from becoming damp.

Ironing

Modern irons have a temperature control which can be set to the appropriate temperature for the fabric you are ironing. (See page 132.)

You can choose a dry or a steam iron. A dry iron is less expensive and can be used with a wet cloth for pressing or for very dry fabrics.

A steam iron is useful for ironing clothes which have become too dry. Other irons spray a fine jet of water over the clothes as they are being ironed. Both steam and spray irons can be used dry instead if you wish.

Looking after the iron
1 Stand the iron on its heel when you are not using it.
2 Don't wind the flex around the iron.
3 Clean the base of the iron with a steel-wool pad if it gets marked.
4 For a steam iron, it is best to use distilled water. This prevents the deposit of 'fur' which could block the steam vents.
5 Empty the water from the iron after use, while it is still hot.

Questions
1 **List six advantages of drying clothes outside.**
2 **Describe how you would use a tumble-drier.**
3 **Suggest five possible ways of getting your washing dry if it was too wet to hang it outside.**
4 **Give five points you would consider carefully before buying an iron.**
5 **How would you care for an iron to keep it in good condition?**

Stain removal

Many everyday stains can be removed by treatment with ordinary washing powders. The treatment depends on:

a the type of stain
b the material which is stained.

1　The first rule with stains is to act quickly before the stain has time to set. Provided the article is washable you should:

   a Put it into cold water (hot water will set the stain).
   b Soak the article (unless unsuitable).
   c Wash as usual.

2　*Removing stains by soaking*

   a Most washing powders contain sodium perborate which removes stains such as tea, coffee or fruit juice. This acts both during soaking in hand-hot water (50°C) and during washing at a high temperature (95°C) if the fabric is suitable.
   b An enzyme (biological) detergent will remove protein stains, e.g. blood, egg, milk or gravy, very effectively during a long soak in warm (40°C) water. After soaking rinse well, then wash in the normal way.

3　*Hypochlorite bleach,* e.g. Domestos, can be used to bleach stains out of white cotton or linen. Never use it undiluted and follow the instructions very carefully. Rinse carefully before washing.

4　*Grease-solvent washing powders* will remove many greasy marks during soaking and washing.

5　*Solvents,* e.g. turpentine, surgical spirit, trichlorethylene (Dabitoff) are used for stubborn greasy or oily stains, or on non-washable articles.
Place a clean white cloth below the stain. Soak another cloth in the solvent and dab at the stain, working from the outside in towards the centre. Rinse well then wash as usual. Air well, if not washable, to remove fumes, and only use solvents in a well-ventilated room.

How to treat some common stains

Blood, egg, milk, gravy	Soak in a warm solution of biological detergent following instructions on the packet. Rinse well, then wash as usual, according to the fabric.
Tea, coffee	Soak in a hand-hot washing powder solution, then wash at the highest temperature suitable for the fabric. If the tea or coffee is milky, soak in a warm solution of biological detergent.
Grass	Treat with methylated spirits or another solvent. Rinse and wash well. *Or* soak in biological detergent, rinse and wash.
Ball-point pen	Treat with methylated spirit or solvent, rinse and wash according to the fabric.
Grease, oil, butter	Soak and wash in grease-solvent washing powder. If not washable, treat with a solvent, and air.
Chewing gum, tar	Scrape off as much as possible, soften the stain by rubbing butter into it and then wipe off with a clean cloth. Remove remaining mark with a solvent then rinse and wash as usual.
Unidentified stains	These are best treated by a professional dry cleaner, if a cold rinse, warm soak and wash does not remove the stain.

Dry cleaning

This is carried out by professional dry cleaners, or in a coin-operated machine at your launderette. It is used for all clothes which cannot be washed. A care-label inside the garment will often have a symbol to advise cleaners as to which particular fluid should be used for cleaning, or to advise against any dry cleaning.

Questions

1 **What are the two main considerations in deciding how to treat a stain?**
2 **If a cup of tea was spilt on a table-cloth, what immediate action would you take?**
3 **How can ordinary washing powders help remove stains?**
4 **What kind of stains do biological detergents remove?**
5 **How would you remove a stain from an article which could not be washed?**
6 **How would you remove the following stains:**
   a gravy from a cotton table-cloth
   b butter or grease from a tea-towel
   c an unidentified stain on an overcoat?

Further work on chapter 6

1 Organize the washing at home for a week. You want good results without spending too much on electricity, detergent, or hot water. At the end of the week, describe how you went about this, and what the results were like.

2 Look at the care labels on some clothes or household textiles. Choose two, and explain the meaning of the symbols in words.

3 Select one washing powder plus two other products that you might use when laundering clothes. Describe the usefulness and cost of each one.

4 You have to deal with the following laundry problems. Say what you would do in each case.
   a A nosebleed on a blue poly-cotton pillowcase.
   b An ink mark on your favourite light-coloured sweater.
   c Food stains on a white pure cotton tee-shirt.

5 You have to take on the responsibility of the weekly family washing as your mother has started a full-time job. What products would you want to keep in the cupboard to deal with this?

Sources of further information

Lever Brothers Education Unit, International Teaching Resource Centre, P O Box 10, Wetherby, West Yorks., LS23 7EH. Many videos, workcards, booklets and leaflets available. Subjects include detergents, care of fabrics, washing machines, care labels, ironing, etc.

Proctor and Gamble Education Service, P O Box 1EE, Gosforth, Newcastle upon Tyne, NE99 1EE. Videos, leaflets, and wallcharts on subjects similar to above.

Home Laundering Consultative Council, 7 Swallow Place, Oxford Circus, London W1R 7AA. Leaflets, handbook, and poster are available.

Books
All about fabrics by Stephanie K. Holland, Oxford University Press.

Fabrics and Laundrywork by Lilian Gawthorpe, Stanley Thornes/Hulton.

Chapter 7

Managing your money

Paying the bills

Careful planning is needed in most households to cover all the necessary expenses and to leave some money for extras. People often take on more expenses than they can afford, especially as so many shops offer easy credit facilities to tempt you to buy. Though it seems easy at first, the money has to be paid eventually, and you nearly always pay more for goods bought on credit (see page 150).

Planning the payment of bills

To help you plan more easily, you can find ways of spreading regular bills, so that you do not have to pay out large sums of money all at once. It may happen that you are paid weekly but many of your bills have to be paid once a month, or once a quarter, or even just once or twice a year. You can make different arrangements for paying most household bills so that you can even out the cost by paying as you go. For example:

Gas and electricity bills

These usually arrive once a quarter but you can easily arrange to pay in a way that suits you better. These ways could include:

1   Paying an agreed amount each week or month. You pay the same amount summer and winter and any extra or under payment is sorted out at the end of the year.
2   You can buy stamps at showrooms, some post offices, and sometimes from agents if you do not live near a showroom.
3   You can have a slot meter if it is safe and practical for one to be fitted. This might mean that your fuel costs a little more, but as you always pay in advance this way, you never have to worry about the bill coming in.
4   You can pay what you like, when you like, off your next bill. If, for example, you work a lot of overtime one week, you can make an extra payment, and pay less when you earn less.

If you expect to have difficulty paying a gas or electricity bill you should let the board know as soon as possible. If you do not pay your bill without explaining why, the supply could be cut off. The bills have to be paid eventually, but you can get advice on easier ways of paying and on 'pay as you go' plans to suit you. You will be advised as to whether or not the D.H.S.S. or Social Services can help you in any way.

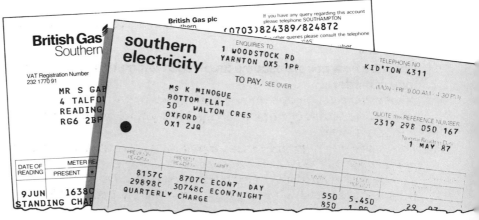

TV licence and telephone bill

You can buy stamps towards these bills at the Post Office and you can pay for the TV licence in instalments through the Post Office Transcash system.

Rent and rates

Rates demands (bills) are sent out once a year, but you can easily arrange to pay in equal monthly instalments. Council and certain other tenants usually pay rates along with the rent. Many people, employed and unemployed, are entitled to housing benefit to help pay rent and rates. You can get details about this from your local council office or Housing Advice Centre.

Mortgages

When someone becomes unemployed it may be very difficult to keep up mortgage payments on a flat or house. You should inform the Building Society straight away as they can sometimes help while you are in difficulty, for example, by extending the number of years you have to pay them back and paying less now. It is better to consult them about this early, rather than to get behind with the payments and possibly to end up losing your home. As this is happening increasingly often nowadays, insurance against this loss of earnings has been introduced and can be arranged for a monthly payment.

Questions

1 **Describe how people become involved in taking on more expenses than they can afford.**
2 **What effects can poor money management have on family life?**
3 **What is the advantage of spreading the payment of regular bills over a period of time?**
4 **Four 'easy-payment' schemes for gas and electricity bills are described here. Which of the four would you use, and why?**
5 **You think you may be entitled to Housing Benefit to help pay your rent and rates. Where is the place to go for information in your area?**

Making a budget

Income

The bills and expenses have to be paid from your income. This could include money from any of these sources:

1 Wages or salary from full- or part-time work. Wages are worked out and paid on a weekly basis, a salary is based on the year and is divided up and paid in 12 equal monthly instalments.
2 Child benefit is paid for each child in the family with an extra allowance for one-parent families.
3 Other benefits from the D.H.S.S., for example, unemployment benefit, income support (formerly supplementary benefit), retirement benefit (see pages 186–7).
4 Contributions for 'keep' from sons or daughters at work or on a training scheme.
5 Money from a paper round, Saturday job, or other casual work.
6 Interest from any savings you have.

Expenses

We have seen that the usual household expenses can include rent or mortgage, rates, food, fuel, H.P. payments, fares, TV rental and licence, insurance, phone, clothing, newspapers, savings, and spending money.

Budgets

Balancing your income and expenses is called making a budget. For example, the budget shown here suggests how one particular family could plan their spending. The father is in full-time work, the mother works a few hours part-time while the two children, aged five and seven, are at school. They rent their home from the local housing corporation and rates are paid in with the rent. They do not have a phone. The father goes to work by bus each day. They make weekly H.P. payments for furniture and a small mail-order catalogue payment for clothing.

Income		Expenses	
Wages for father's work (after deductions for tax, National Insurance, etc.)	£...	Rent and rates(about 20%	£...
		Gas and electricity	£...
		Food	£...
Wages for mother's part-time work	£...	H.P. on furniture	£...
		TV rental and licence	£...
Child benefit	£...	Insurance	£...
		Clothing from mail order catalogue	£...
		Money left for 'extras'	£...
Total	£...	Total	£...

Your own budget

While you are still at school you will probably have only yourself to spend your money on. Work out how much money you might expect to receive; it might vary a lot from one week to another. You may receive extra at Christmas or on birthdays. You may earn extra occasionally by doing odd jobs for people, for example, babysitting, gardening, cleaning cars, etc.

Perhaps you have a fixed amount of pocket money or an allowance. You may have a part-time job, such as delivering papers or milk, or working in a shop.

Spending

Write down how you use your money each week. Try and work out how much you spend on different things like clothes, records or tapes, fares, eating out, chocolate and sweets, drinks, magazines, going out, saving.

Leaving school

When you leave school you will hope to start a job, a training scheme, or receive Income Support (formerly Supplementary Benefit). Your expenses will probably change then as well as your income. If you earn a wage you will have to pay tax and National Insurance. You will probably need to pay for fares and lunches. You may have to buy clothes for work that you would not normally wear. You will probably pay something to your parents towards the cost of your keep.

Questions

1 **What is a budget?**
2 **Why is it useful for a family to draw up a budget?**
3 **Draw up a budget for an imaginary family (or one you know, if you like). It can be either for a week or a month. Describe a different household from the one above, saying who is in the family, their ages, if they are at work, at home, or at school. Write down where their income comes from and how much it is. Then list all their expenses. Draw up a suitable budget, on the lines of the one above, making sure it balances. Work it out roughly at first; when you have got it to balance, draw up a neat copy.**
4 **Draw up a budget for yourself to see what your income and spending might be in an average sort of week.**
5 **Write down the sort of work or training scheme you would like to start when you leave school. What expenses would that involve you in that you do not have now?**

Bank accounts

Where to open a bank account

The main clearing banks in this country are Lloyds, Barclays, Midland, National Westminster, the Trustee Savings Bank, and the Royal Bank of Scotland. Other well established banks include the Yorkshire Bank, the Co-operative bank, and the National Girobank run by the Post Office. All of these offer a wide range of financial services, sometimes at lower charges than the clearing banks. Some of them are open for longer hours than the clearing banks too, and this makes it much easier to visit them. Some Building Societies also offer a range of banking services.

As most of these places are now competing for you to open an account with them, they are improving the services they offer all the time. Because of this, you should look carefully at what each one offers before deciding where to open your account.

Some of the services which banks can offer

1   You are given a cheque book with your name on each cheque and a cheque guarantee card (see p. 146). This means you don't have to carry large sums of money around with you for shopping or for paying bills.
2   Banking is usually free if you keep your account in credit (i.e. keep some money in it). But if you become overdrawn, the charges for carrying out any transaction can be quite high.
3   Your wages or salary can be paid straight into your bank account by your employer. You receive a payslip telling you what you have earned.
4   To keep a record of how much money you have, the bank sends you a statement at regular intervals. It shows what has been paid in, what has been withdrawn, and any charges the bank has made.
5   If you wish, the bank will pay your regular bills for you direct from your account by means of a standing order or direct debit, for example, for your rent or your TV rental.
6   You can apply for a mortgage from most banks (except the Girobank) to buy a house or flat at the usual rate of interest.
7   You can get a bank loan for large expenses like a car or home improvements.
8   You can open a deposit account for savings if you want to. You earn interest on the money in a deposit account.
9   They will arrange traveller's cheques and foreign currency for visits abroad.
10 They have cash dispensers for 'out of hours' withdrawals and other services.

Building societies offering banking services

Building societies no longer only offer savings accounts and lend money to buy houses. They now provide several banking services. For example, the Halifax Building Society has a Cardcash Account which offers many of the services once only available through a current account at a bank, including the following:
1   Use of a plastic cashcard and a personal number known only to you to use in a 'through the wall' cash dispenser open 18 hours a day or over the counter. You can pay in or draw out cash and ask for a statement.

2   Your salary can be paid straight into your account by your employer so that it earns interest for you.

3   Your household bills like gas, phone, or rates can be paid, either by free standing orders for equal instalments spread through the year, or in full as they come in, again free of charge.

It is worth considering an account of this kind if you are thinking of opening a bank account. The main advantage, of course, is that you receive interest on the money in your Cardcash account while all the services are free. The main disadvantage with some of the societies is that you may not have a cheque book for shopping.

Points to help you decide where to open a bank account:

1   Is there a branch convenient for where you work or live?
2   Will the opening hours be suitable for you to visit?
3   What will the charges be if you overdraw?
4   Do they pay any interest on money in your account?
5   Opening free gifts may be worth having – money, pens, etc. If the normal services they offer will suit you, you may as well take advantage of such gifts.

Questions

1   **There are several advantages in having a bank account for everyday use. If you were at work, which two would be most useful to you?**
2   **In the area where you live, which of the above named banks has a branch?**
3   **Which banks are likely to have longer opening hours?**
4   **Where do you find branches of the Girobank?**
5   **Do you pay bank charges on a current account at a clearing bank?**

Current accounts

The usual type of account that most customers have is called a <u>current account</u> (or <u>cheque account</u> at the T.S.B.). You are not paid any interest on the money you have in a current account. You are given a cheque book and the account works in this way:

To pay money in You fill in a slip and hand it over the counter with the money or cheque.

To take money out You are given a cheque book with your name printed on each cheque. If you want cash, you write out a cheque to yourself and receive the money over the counter. Many branches have a cash dispenser in the outside wall which you can use when the bank is closed. You insert a special cash card and tap in your personal number to receive the cash.

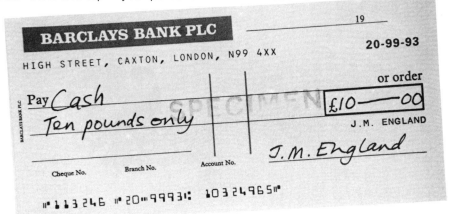

To pay by cheque, for example, at a shop. You write out the cheque, sign it, and give it to the person you are paying. They will usually ask to see your Cheque Guarantee Card and will write its number on the back of the cheque. This is the shop's guarantee that they will receive the money due to them, up to a certain amount (£50 at present), even if you have no money in your account to cover it. The bank will only give you a cheque guarantee card if you have shown that you are a reliable person who does not keep writing out cheques when there is not enough money in your account to cover them. Sometimes you can make an arrangement with a bank for an overdraft. This means you are allowed to draw more money out of your account than you have in it, up to an agreed amount. You have to pay them interest on this money, as it is like taking out a loan.

If you are out shopping and want to buy a pair of shoes costing £18 from a shop called Shoeline, this is how you would fill in the cheque. You also fill in the counterfoil as your own record of what you have spent.

Debit cards
The Barclays Connect card is a debit card which is used instead of a cheque. When buying goods in a shop you simply sign the sales voucher and the cost is debited from your current account. Unlike a cheque guarantee card, which has a limit of £50, the debit card allows you to buy goods of any price, providing the money is available in your account. Remember that it is *not* a credit card.

Bank statements

The bank gives you a statement, usually once a month, as a record of all the money that has gone in or out of the account.

		DEBIT	CREDIT	BALANCE
MARCH 1987	Bartons Bank PLC			
Name of account: Jane Smith	Reid Rd. Branch			
Account Number: 0147326	Merley			
DATE DETAILS				127.43 C
MAR. 1 Bal. Brought Forward				104.48 C
3 515420		22.95		90.26 C
5 515421		14.22		290.26 C
8 Littlewoods			200.00	278.26 C
11 Gen. Acc. Insurance S.O.		12.00		263.03 C
13 515423		15.23		255.44 C
14 514422		7.59		245.00 C
15 Charges to March 8		10.44		295.87 C
16 Sundries			50.87	171.87 C
20 Nat. Build. Society S.O.		124.00		141.27 C
22 Merley Council		30.60		3.73 D
24 Sunshine Holidays		145.00		47.14 C
25 Sundries			50.87	47.14 C
31 Carried forward				

ABBREVIATIONS

S.O.	Standing order	Ch.	Charges	C Credit balance
D.D.	Direct Debit	Ad.	Already Advised	D Debit balance

Questions

1 **Draw a diagram of a cheque made out to British Gas for £32.65, signed by yourself.**
2 **Look at the statement above and see if you can work out:**
   a How much was in the account on 5 March?
   b How does Jane Smith pay for her insurance?
   c Who do you think she works for?
   d What do you think the entry on 20 March might be?
   e What happened on 24 March and 25 March?

Saving

It is always useful to be able to save some money for a special item or holiday, or for an unexpected expense. Although you could keep your money at home for bills you are soon going to pay, it is not a good idea to keep money in the house for any long period. You could be tempted to spend it, or you could lose it all if your house was broken into. Also, money kept at home does not earn interest for you, whereas nearly all saving schemes give you interest on the money you save. Interest is the amount your money earns for you at the end of the year. For example, if you had £100 in the bank and it earned 10% interest per year you would have £110 by the end of a year. If the money earned 5% interest you would have £105 by the end of the year.

How do you choose?

There are many kinds of saving schemes available; it will pay you to look around carefully before you decide what is best for you. Many of the banks and building societies have special offers to encourage young people to open an account with them. They may offer free pens, sports bags, money boxes, vouchers, and so on. These are often attractive offers which are worth having, but there are other points to consider as well, especially if you are trying to save more seriously.

1 Is there a branch of the building society, bank or Post Office near where you live, work, or go to school?

2 What are the opening hours? You do not want to choose somewhere that is always closed at the times you can go there.

Bank hours are normally 9.30 to 3.30 only, Monday to Friday. A few branches of some banks may be open at extra times, including Saturday mornings.

Post Offices, building societies and the T.S.B. are usually open longer hours; until 5 p.m. or 5.30, and often on Saturday mornings as well.

3 How much interest will they pay you? It varies quite a lot from place to place so check very carefully. If you are not saving large amounts for a long time this may not be very important to you.

4 How easily can you get your money out when you want to? Do you have to give them notice?
5 How seriously are you saving? For a pair of shoes, a holiday, or the deposit on a house?

Some different ways of saving

1 *With a building society* They give a good rate of interest. If you are saving for the deposit on a house or flat this could be the best way to do it as a building society is much more likely to lend you the money to buy a house if you have saved with it regularly.
2 *In a deposit account at a bank* They offer a reasonable rate of interest though their opening hours are shorter. Banks also offer mortgages so it could suit you to save with them for this reason.
3 *Trustee Savings Banks (T.S.B.)* offer a reasonable rate of interest and have more branches and longer opening hours than most banks. Again, as they give priority for mortgages to their own savers, it might suit you to save with them if you are saving for a mortgage.
4 *Post offices* Their many schemes include ordinary and investment accounts. They have many branches, but the ordinary account gives only a low rate of interest. The investment account gives a much higher rate, and is especially good for people who do not pay any income tax, but you do have to give a month's notice to withdraw your money.
   Premium Bonds are bought in £5 units from post offices. You are not paid interest but you have the chance of winning a money prize of between £50 and £250,000 from thousands of prizes drawn every week.

Questions
1 **Name five places near where you live where you could keep your savings.**
2 **Say how you would advise someone to save for each of the following and why it is a suitable choice:**
   a spending money for an outing in a month's time
   b a cassette player
   c the deposit on a flat you would like to buy.
3 **Of the schemes described above, which**
   a gives no interest
   b gives a particularly low rate of interest
   c is a good choice for people who pay no income tax?

Buying on credit

There are several ways of buying on credit, including hire-purchase (see page 152), shopping accounts in stores, mail order catalogues, credit cards, and personal loans from banks. 'Credit' means that you have the goods straight away, using borrowed money to pay, and you pay it off later in instalments, paying extra in interest. It may at first seem much easier to buy this way rather than by saving up and paying in cash all at once but there are disadvantages to credit, which you should think about carefully.

1   You usually pay more for credit than if you pay cash because of the interest charges. For example, a £100 coat might cost £130 if you buy it on credit. Sometimes a shop has an interest free credit offer, and this can be worth considering.

2   If you have cash, you can shop around for the best price for what you want, rather than having to shop only where credit terms are offered.

3   It is very easy to be tempted to take on more payments than you can really afford. Once you get behind with them, debts can mount up very quickly. Shops and stores do not normally check that you can afford the repayments because their main interest is in selling something to you. It is up to you to control your own credit buying and to keep it within reasonable limits.

A.P.R.

When you want to compare the real cost of buying on credit in different places you should look for the A.P.R. This is the Annual Percentage Rate of interest and must, by law, be shown on all advertisements for credit or loans. It shows you the true cost because it has to take into account the amount of (a) the interest charged (b) any compulsory 'one-off' charges, such as a charge for arranging the credit or loan (c) the cost of losing any discount there might have been if you had paid cash. For example, in one particular week the A.P.R. on various schemes for credit or loans was shown as:

B.H.S. Budget Account	32.1%	Access Card	26.8%
H.P. through Electricity Board	36.0%	Boots Personal Loan	29.9%
John Lewis Stores Option Account	21.6%	Lloyds Bank Personal Loan	23.1%

Of course, these charges can vary from time to time, but it pays you to know that these differences exist, so that you can look around and get the best possible terms if you decide to buy on credit.

Mail order credit

This is quite a popular way of buying on credit. An agent keeps a catalogue and you choose goods (clothes, toys, household goods, etc.) from it in your own home. The agent orders the goods for you and you pay the agent a certain amount each week until they are paid off. If for any reason you don't want to keep the goods, the agent will send them back for you post-free. The agent receives about 10% commision on all the goods she sells. (Most agents are women.) For example, if she sells goods worth £100, she may be allowed £10 worth of goods free for herself. Mail-order buying is useful because you can spread the cost over several weeks and you don't have to pay the full cost at once. But you can usually buy the goods cheaper in the shops so it costs more in the end, like most credit buying.

Department store and shop accounts

Most stores now offer credit accounts, for example, Marks and Spencer, Littlewoods, and Boots. They encourage customers to shop at that store rather than any other and make it easier for them to do so. The account usually allows you to pay for your goods in monthly instalments if you wish, up to a credit limit which you and the store have previously agreed. You pay interest on what you owe the store at the end of the month.

Credit cards

Examples of these are the Access card and the Barclaycard. (You do not need an account at Barclays Bank to have a Barclaycard.) You apply to the bank for a card and they agree to allow you a certain credit limit. You can use the card to pay bills in shops, garages, restaurants, hotels, and to pay train and air fares. You can also use it abroad wherever you see the sign displayed. Instead of paying for goods in cash, you give them your card to check and you sign for the goods. Later in the month Barclaycard or Access send you a statement telling you how much you owe them. Then you either pay them at once in full and pay no interest (one of the few times when credit is free), or you can spread the re-payments over a period of time and pay an interest charge.

Questions

1　**What is**
　　a　the main advantage and
　　b　the main disadvantage of buying goods on credit?
2　**You want to buy a certain item costing £100 on credit. Of the places named above, which would be**
　　a　the cheapest place and
　　b　the most expensive place to buy?
　　Say what the total credit price would include in each case.
3　**Why do you think that many people enjoy buying from mail order catalogues?**
4　**Why do large stores encourage customers to open credit accounts?**
5　**List the kind of places where people often pay by credit card.**

Hire-purchase

Hire-purchase (H.P.) is one way of buying on credit. It can be useful for large, essential items that would take a long time to save for, such as furniture or a car. It is better to use hire-purchase only to buy goods you need, not those you would just like to have. You must be careful not to buy so much on H.P. that your weekly payments become difficult to keep up.

Remember these important points when you buy anything on hire-purchase:

1   The goods do not belong to you until you have made the very last payment.

2   If you have paid more than one-third of the price, and you fall behind with the payments, the dealer cannot take them away from you without a court order. You will still have to pay for them, but the court will decide how much you have to pay, and how often.

3   If a salesman comes to your home and you sign an agreement there, the law allows you three days to change your mind after signing. This is because the law recognizes that you are more likely to be talked into buying goods you don't really need when you are in your own home rather than in a shop. If you have paid a deposit, you are entitled to have it returned to you.

4   You will pay more for goods bought on credit. If, for example, you buy a gas cooker which costs £300 cash, you may have to pay about £360 to buy it on hire-purchase, because you have to pay interest charges. The rate of interest varies between one shop and another, so shop around for the best rate. Large stores and electricity boards often charge lower rates of interest than small shops. When you go to buy the item, the shop must tell you the cash price, the A.P.R., and the total hire-purchase price so that you will realize how much extra it will cost you to buy it on hire-purchase.

5   If you have any complaints about goods bought on H.P., you must take them up with the finance company you have the H.P. agreement with, not the shop where you bought the goods as is normally the case.

6   If you read the hire-purchase agreement and find it difficult to understand, or find it difficult to keep up payments, you can get free advice from the Citizens' Advice Bureau. This exists to help people with any problems like this – legal, financial or about consumer affairs. They are there to help all citizens, free of charge. Their address is always in the phone book.

Questions

1   **What are the advantages of buying on hire-purchase?**
2   **Why shouldn't you buy too much on hire-purchase?**
3   **Why do you pay more for goods bought on hire-purchase?**
4   **You are thinking of buying a washing machine on hire-purchase. What are the most important points to remember?**
5   **How can you get help in understanding hire-purchase agreements?**
6   **How would you find the Citizens' Advice Bureau in your area?**

Insurance

Insurance provides you with financial security in case of unexpected events or losses. The principle behind all insurance is that you make regular payments to an insurance company as a safeguard against certain events which could happen to you, such as fire, theft, or a car accident. If this event should happen, then the insurance company will pay you a previously agreed amount of money to help compensate you for the loss or damage.

There are many insurance companies in business. You will find their offices in any high street or shopping centre. They offer many kinds of different insurance.

Life assurance

It is a good idea for breadwinners in the family to take out Life Assurance policies. This makes sure that the family will be provided for if either of them should die. They can arrange for a mortgage protection policy to pay off the mortgage in case of death, so that the family will still have a home.

House insurance

Buildings

If you borrow money to buy a house, the building society (or whoever lends you the money) will insist that you insure the house against fire or other damage, so that their property is protected. As house values usually increase over the years, you must review the amount for which the house is insured every year.

Contents

It is in your own interest to insure the contents of your house – furniture, equipment, carpets, electrical items, and so on – against accidents such as fire, theft, or flood. The premium you pay depends on the value of your belongings. You pay so much for every £100 worth of goods. Large or expensive items, like furs or jewellery, should be insured separately.

There are basically two different ways of insuring your house:

1   You insure the contents for their current value. If you make a claim the insurance company will not give you the price you paid for an article when it was new, but will reduce this to the amount they consider it was worth when it was damaged or stolen, perhaps after several years wear and tear. This means that you would be very unlikely to receive enough money to buy a new item to replace the one you lost.
2   You can insure your household goods so that you receive the full amount it would cost you to replace them. The premium for this kind of insurance will be higher.

Crime prevention

No insurance can really make up for your home being burgled, so take precautions. Burglaries are on the increase, especially in cities, so it is important to make your home as secure as possible. You can ask at your local police station for a free visit from the Crime Prevention Officer who will advise you on how to improve your home security.

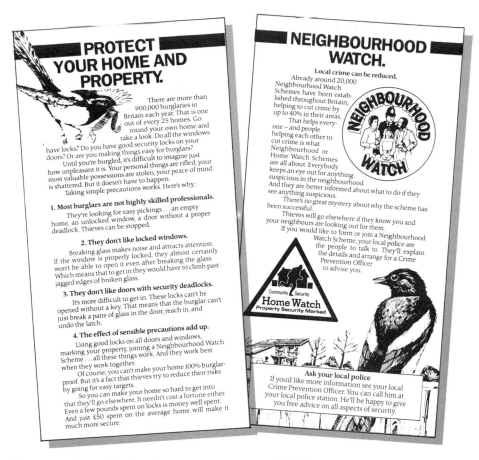

PROTECT YOUR HOME AND PROPERTY.

There are more than 900,000 burglaries in Britain each year. That is one out of every 25 homes. Go round your own home and take a look. Do all the windows have locks? Do you have good security locks on your doors? Or are you making things easy for burglars?

Until you're burgled, it's difficult to imagine just how unpleasant it is. Your personal things are rifled, your most valuable possessions are stolen, your peace of mind is shattered. But it doesn't have to happen. Taking simple precautions works. Here's why:

1. Most burglars are not highly skilled professionals.

They're looking for easy pickings... an empty home, an unlocked window, a door without a proper deadlock. Thieves can be stopped.

2. They don't like locked windows.

Breaking glass makes noise and attracts attention. If the window is properly locked, they almost certainly won't be able to open it even after breaking the glass. Which means that to get in they would have to climb past jagged edges of broken glass.

3. They don't like doors with security deadlocks.

It's more difficult to get in. These locks can't be opened without a key. That means that the burglar can't just break a pane of glass in the door, reach in, and undo the latch.

4. The effect of sensible precautions add up.

Using good locks on all doors and windows, marking your property, joining a Neighbourhood Watch Scheme... all these things work. And they work best when they work together.

Of course, you can't make your home 100% burglar-proof. But it's a fact that thieves try to reduce their risks by going for easy targets.

So you can make your home so hard to get into that they'll go elsewhere. It needn't cost a fortune either. Even a few pounds spent on locks is money well spent. And just £50 spent on the average home will make it much more secure.

NEIGHBOURHOOD WATCH.

Local crime can be reduced. Already around 20,000 Neighbourhood Watch Schemes have been established throughout Britain, helping to cut crime by up to 40% in their areas.

That helps everyone – and people helping each other to cut crime is what Neighbourhood or Home Watch Schemes are all about. Everybody keeps an eye out for anything suspicious in the neighbourhood. And they are better informed about what to do if they see anything suspicious.

There's no great mystery about why the scheme has been successful.

Thieves will go elsewhere if they know you and your neighbours are looking out for them.

If you would like to form or join a Neighbourhood Watch Scheme, your local police are the people to talk to. They'll explain the details and arrange for a Crime Prevention Officer to advise you.

Community Security Home Watch Property Security Marked

Ask your local police

If you'd like more information see your local Crime Prevention Officer. You can call him at your local police station. He'll be happy to give you free advice on all aspects of security.

Here are a few of the basic measures you could take:

1 Fit good deadlocks on your front and back doors; the Yale type locks can be broken quite easily by intruders. Bolts on the door are a good idea, as are door chains, so that you can see who is at the door before you open it. An outside light helps too.
2 Windows on the ground floor or those that can be reached by a flat roof or drainpipe should have windowlocks fitted and used.
3 When you leave your house or go to bed at night make sure doors and windows are fastened securely.
4 When you go away on holiday, don't forget to cancel the milk and papers. Inform the police and a neighbour whom you can trust so that they can keep an eye on the house for you. But don't let everyone in the neighbourhood know that the house will be empty.

Questions

1 **What is the general purpose of all insurance?**
2 **Why should a couple with a family always take out a Life Assurance policy if they decide to buy a home?**
3 **Why does a Building Society or bank insist that you take out a house insurance policy if they lend you the money to buy a house?**
4 **Think about your living room at home. Work out how much it would cost you to replace everything in it, new.**

Advertising

You are protected against untrue or misleading advertisements by the Trade Descriptions Act of 1968, which makes it illegal for any advertisement, label or spoken statement to mislead people.

But you must protect yourself against adverts which try to persuade you that you need certain goods.

Advertising is big business. Many firms spend a great deal of money employing advertising companies to think up advertisements for their products, to persuade you to part with your money to buy their goods.

Everywhere we go we see advertisements tempting us to spend money. They are on television and radio, at the cinema, on posters, in magazines, and on leaflets pushed through our letter boxes.

Benefits

Advertising does have some benefits. If it increases sales for the manufacturer of the goods it will increase their profits and keep the company in business. For the consumer it has benefits too. It can introduce us to new products that we may like to try and often use anyway, for example, toothpaste, breakfast cereal, shampoo. We may change through advertising to a brand we like better, perhaps to a fluoride toothpaste, or a high-fibre breakfast cereal.

It can make 'money-off' offers or give you free samples to encourage you to try the goods. It can keep prices down, for example, adverts keep down the cost of buying newspapers and magazines. The 'free' newspapers that come through our doors are paid for by the people and firms placing advertisements in them.

Disadvantages

Although advertising has these benefits, it does have some disadvantages too. If people, particularly young people and children, are persuaded by advertising that they want or need something the family cannot afford, they may feel discontented and resentful because they cannot have the goods.

Advertisements usually show us people who are smarter, more good-looking, better dressed, living in better houses, and having more fun than the ordinary people that most of us are. They can make us want to be like them. We may associate the products being advertised with the kind of life they show and think that buying the products will make us more like these perfect people. Often we are hardly aware that we are reacting in this way. But remember that if you do buy the product, you are only getting a bar of soap, a box of chocolates, or a bottle of shampoo. So look out for clever advertising and try to decide for yourself what you really need and how to get the best value for your money.

The Advertising Standards Authority

The A.S.A. acts as a public watchdog on advertising. It tries to ensure that all advertising is 'legal, decent, honest, and truthful'. It was set up by members of the advertising industry to protect their own reputation.

What does it do? It has a code of practice or set of rules which most advertisers have agreed to follow. If an advertiser produces an advert which is not considered 'legal, decent, honest and truthful', he/she is asked to change it to bring it into line. The fear of bad publicity usually ensures that this is done.

DO ADVERTISEMENTS SOMETIMES DISTORT THE TRUTH?

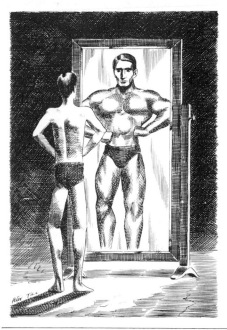

The Advertising ✓
Standards Authority.
If an advertisement is wrong,
we're here to put it right.

ASA Ltd, Brook House,
Torrington Place, London WC1E 7HN.

What does it cover? It covers advertisements in newspapers, magazines, leaflets, posters, and on wrapped goods. For example, one of the A.S.A.'s many cases dealt with a pizza restaurant which had advertised in the local paper 'extra dishes half price'. Someone who visited this restaurant to try this offer was told that it applied to children's meals only. He complained to the A.S.A. that the advert was unfair and misleading. The A.S.A. upheld his complaint and the restaurant agreed not to repeat the advert.

The A.S.A. cannot check every one of the thousands of advertisements and sales promotions which appear, so it likes to hear from the public about any that are felt to be unfair and will investigate them. The address of the A.S.A. is shown above.

Questions

1 **Which law was passed to prevent advertisers from making untrue claims?**
2 **Describe one important way in which advertising could benefit**
   a the advertiser and
   b the consumer.
3 **Why might parents object to some of the advertising aimed at young children?**
4 **Describe an advert now being shown on television which is aimed at people your own age. Why do you think it is likely to make you want to try the product?**
5 **What is the main purpose of the Advertising Standards Authority?**

Labelling schemes

You will often find labels attached to goods when you go shopping. Many of these labels are a sign of quality and reliability. They will only be attached to goods which have passed careful tests for safety and quality.

You will find these labels attached to a variety of goods, including gas and electrical appliances. When you see them, you will know that the goods are worth buying.

Here are some of the labels you should look out for.

The B.S.I. (British Standards Institution) tests a wide variety of goods sent to them by manufacturers. They carry out strict tests on the goods for quality, durability and safety. Only those products which meet the high standards of the B.S.I. are allowed to have the Kitemark attached to them.

This means that when you see any article in the shops which displays the Kitemark you can be confident that it will be a well-made product of reliable quality. Many different products carry the Kitemark, including babies' cots, crash helmets, paint, car windscreens and seat belts.

Either or both of these labels may be attached to gas appliances such as cookers and gas fires as a mark of safety and quality.

The B.E.A.B. (British Electrotechnical Approvals Board) also has its own safety mark attached to or engraved on electrical appliances, including cookers, hairdriers and irons.

Pure New Wool is a high quality material which is often imitated. When you see this label attached to garments or fabrics you can be certain that it really is wool that is:

Pure new wool

Pure — not mixed with any other fibre.

New — not wool that has been used before and recycled.

Oil heaters have caused many fires. The only safe kind to buy are those which are marked with this sign. This means that the heater
a has a reliable guard
b cannot be knocked over easily and
c has a device to ensure that the flame will go out if it should accidentally be knocked over.

The Design Council has a permanent exhibition of well-designed British-made goods. If an article is 'well designed' it means that it is well made from good quality material, suitable for the purpose it is meant for and pleasing in appearance.

Goods selected by the Design Centre can display this mark as a sign of good design and quality. You may see it attached to furniture, cutlery and tableware, toys and many other household goods.

Questions

1 **When you go shopping, what is the point of looking for labels attached to goods?**

2 **Draw the labels you would expect to find attached to the following:**
   a an electric sewing machine or power drill
   b a gas central heating boiler
   c a coffee table
   d a winter skirt or jumper
   e a portable oil heater.
   Beside each label write down what it would tell you about the article it was attached to.

Consumer protection

There are many laws and organizations which exist to protect the rights and interests of consumers or shoppers.

You ought to know your legal rights when you go shopping so that you can make sure you always get good value for your money.

Here are just two of the many laws which have been passed to make sure that everyone can get a fair deal when they are shopping.

The Sale of Goods Act, 1893

This says that:

a All goods must be fit to be sold, that is, they must be of good enough quality to work properly. For example, clothes must not come apart when you wear them. Electrical goods must work.

b They must be suitable for the purpose for which you buy them. Discuss with the shopkeeper the use you are going to make of the goods, then it is his responsibility to sell you only something suitable.

c All goods must be as they are labelled or described.

So if you buy a pair of shoes and they come apart at the seams after a week's wear, you should take them back to the shop.

The shop must either change them or refund your money. It is the responsibility of the shopkeeper to do this, not the manufacturer of the goods. He must keep the law, so politely insist on your legal rights.

The Trade Descriptions Act 1968

This makes it illegal for any labels, advertisements or spoken statements to mislead customers.

For example, if you book a holiday in a caravan 'with beautiful views of the sea, only one minute from the beach', then this must actually be true.

Sale bargains

If you buy a sale article which says it is 'reduced from £10 to £4', it must really have been on sale for £10 for at least 28 days out of the last six months.

Guarantees

Sometimes in the past, if you signed a guarantee, you signed away your legal rights without realizing it.

But now there is a law which prevents manufacturers of goods from getting out of their obligations, that is, to provide you with goods that are:

a fit for sale.

b fit for the purpose they are sold for.

c just as they have been advertised.

Now, no guarantee can take away your legal rights. Sometimes it adds to your normal rights, so it is worth signing. Often it is the quickest way of getting any faulty new equipment put right.

Extended guarantees

Many manufacturers now offer extended guarantees. You pay an extra sum when you buy the goods and all repairs are free for the extended period, perhaps five years. The cost can be quite high and depends on what you are buying; perhaps on a colour television it would be an extra £50, on an electric food mixer £15.

Only you can decide whether to pay the extra and have no worries about repair costs for five years, or whether to hope for the best and have no major repairs at that time, therefore saving yourself the money. You need to bear in mind that the cost of a 'service visit' can be quite high, even before you pay for any parts.

Questions

1 **Why do you think everyone should know their legal rights when shopping?**
2 **What are the three main provisions of the Sale of Goods Act?**
3 **If you bought a new coat, and the stitching came undone the first time you wore it, what would you do?**
4 **How is the Trade Descriptions Act useful?**
5 **If you bought a new washing machine would you bother to sign and send off the guarantee that came with it? Why?**
6 **If you were buying a new video recorder for £500 and the cost of extending the guarantee to five years was £55, would you pay the extra cost for this? Give your reasons.**

Consumer advice

The Consumers' Association

This is an independent association formed to give information and advice to consumers.

It publishes a magazine called *Which?*. You can take out a regular subscription to this, or look at it in your local library.

Stereo radio recorders

	target price (£)	size and weight (kg)	battery cost	general features	radio: FM reception	FM sound quality	AM wavebands	AM reception	AM sound quality	SW	features	cassette: sound quality	copying	built-in mics	features
Aiwa CS-W300 [10] (Singapore)	70	II	£	ADF			LMS				PQ				bdnpq
Akai PJ-R25 (Japan)	130	IIII	£££	ABCEFGH [1]			LMS				NPQR		N/A	N/A	bcdel
Deccasound DSC 1123 (Taiwan)	70	II	£££	ADF	[2]		LM	[2]		N/A	NP				bdknpr
Fisher PH-W 546 (Korea)	80	II	£	ADG			LMS				KPQ				dglnpqr
Grundig RR1500 (Singapore)	110	II	££	ADFH			LMS				PQ				bdknpq
Hitachi TRK-3D2 (Singapore)	100	III	£	AEFH [1]			LMS				PQ		N/A		dkn
Hitachi TRK-W24 (Singapore)	80	III	££	ADH [1]			LMS				PQ				bdknpr
ITT Weekend 360 (Malaysia)	100	III	££	ADFH [3]			LMS				PQ				bdknp
JVC RC-W3LB [4] (Japan)	100	II	££££	ADH			LMS				KPQ				bdimnpqr
Omega EL-9052 (China)	65	III	££	ABDFGH			LMS				PQ				bdknp
Panasonic RX-FW17L (Japan)	80	II	£	ACD			LMS				KPQ				dgnpqr
Philips D8334 [5] (Japan)	80	III	£	ACDFH			LMS				PQ		N/A		cdgknpr
Realistic SCR-51 [6] (Taiwan)	90	II	££	ACDFG			LM			N/A	PQ				bdkn
Saisho T808 [7] (Korea)	70	III	££	ABCD			LMS				KPQ		N/A		bdgkn
Sanyo M-S350L (Japan)	110	I	£££	ABDGJ			M				N/A		N/A		beln
Sony CFS-950 (Japan)	130	II	£££	ADG			LMS				KQ			N/A	bdg[8]p
Sony CFS-W30L [4] (Korea)	70	II	£	AE			LM				N/A PQ		N/A		bdgn
Sunkyong SRC-2100 (Korea)	50	II	£££				LMS								bdnpqr
Toshiba RT 8055 [9] (Japan)	90	II	£££	ADFH [1]			LMS				Q				

[1] Inputs only
[2] Set not available in time for these tests
[3] Outputs only
[4] Discontinued but may still be in some shops
[5] Being replaced by D8186 – see Box
[6] From Tandy shops only
[7] Being replaced by Saisho PT220 – similar performance but detachable speakers and lacking features C.L.P.bknr. Both from Dixons and Power City only
[8] Both decks
[9] Being replaced by RT 8036 – see Box
[10] Being replaced by CS-W220 – see Box. Has feature r but lacks F, P, b

Key
General features
A = headphone socket
B = sockets for external speakers
C = stereo widening switch
D = tone control
E = graphic equaliser
F = balance control
G = can work off external DC supply (eg car battery with adapter)
H = input/output sockets for connecting other audio equipment
J = clock with radio alarm

Radio
K = short wave fine tuning
N = tuning indicator
P = stereo indicator
Q = stereo/mono switch
R = socket for external FM aerial
AM wavebands
L = long wave
M = medium wave
S = short wave (approx 6-18 MHz, 49-16 metres)
Cassette
b = socket(s) for one or two external microphones
c = autostop from fast wind
d = autostop from play/record
e = auto reverse
g = cue and review

k = tape counter
l = programme search
m = microphone mixing (with control for microphone sound level)
n = built-in microphone(s)
p = two cassette decks for copying
n = double-speed copying
r = continuous/relay play
Size and weight
I = smallest/lightest
IIII = biggest/heaviest

KEY TO RATINGS	best ←				→ worst

Stereo radio recorders picked out in coloured bands in the Table are recommended in the Buying Guide.

Stereo radio recorders *Which? December 1986*

The purpose of *Which?* is to provide useful information about a very wide range of goods, to help you always to get the best possible value for money.

Representatives of the Consumers' Association go shopping in the normal way and buy and test all kinds of goods, from cars to cosmetics, from sausages to washing up liquid, from grocery prices to washing machines.

They carefully test all the goods they buy to see if they are:

safe
good value for money
well made
durable
easy to service
reliable.

They tell you what to look out for when you buy certain items. Often they will recommend a 'best-buy'. They can save you from making expensive mistakes.

Consumer Advice Centres

Consumer Advice Centres are run by local councils and are paid for out of the rates. They are usually in shopping centres or High Streets, or there are mobile centres which visit different areas. They offer help of various kinds:

1 As there are so many complicated laws and organizations dealing with consumer affairs they will help you sort out what you need to know or do in any individual case. For example the government Office of Fair Trading watches over and updates the law relating to trading and publishes information booklets. Local Authorities deal with food hygiene laws, the Ministry of Agriculture, Fisheries, and Food deals with food labelling.
2 If you have a complaint about faulty goods or services they will help you to resolve it.
3 They have a wide range of booklets about all aspects of consumer affairs.
4 If you are thinking of buying an expensive item like a second-hand car or a new cooker they will advise you about what to look for.

The Citizens' Advice Bureau

The Citizens' Advice Bureau provides a very useful service. The service is run and paid for by local authorities, often with unpaid voluntary helpers. They will advise you, free of charge and in confidence, on almost any matter.

If you have problems as a consumer – for example, if you have difficulty with shops who refuse to replace shoddy goods and you feel you have not been fairly treated, you can go to your Citizens' Advice Bureau for advice.

Here are just a few of the many problems they can help you with:
Consumer affairs, your rights as a shopper
Legal problems, about insurance, pensions, Social Security, taxation
Personal matters, wills, marriage, divorce, housing, neighbours
Information about places and events
Jobs, training, evening classes

They have offices in most large towns and cities. You can find their address in the local phone book.

Questions
1 **What is the name of the magazine published by the Consumers' Association?**
2 **What is the purpose of the magazine?**
3 **You are thinking about buying a new cooker, but are confused by all the different models that are for sale. Where can you find information about the good and bad points of each?**
4 **If you were thinking of buying a washing machine, what are some of the points you would want to know about it?**
5 **Does the Citizens' Advice Bureau charge you for their advice?**
6 **If a shopkeeper refused to replace a pair of shoes which split the first time you wore them, what could you do?**

Places to shop

Hypermarkets are the newest kind of shopping development. You can buy a great variety of goods under one roof, not only food, but furniture, clothes, electrical, and most other goods. Sometimes there is also a small bank, separate, small, specialist shops, and a cafeteria. Hypermarkets are usually built on the outskirts of a town, well away from the centre so they have the great advantage of plenty of parking space near to the store.

Chain stores such as British Home Stores, Littlewoods, Woolworth, Marks and Spencer. You get the same kind of goods and prices in every one of their stores and a standard of quality that is always similar so that you can rely on it. Most offer credit facilities if you open an account with them. (See page 151.)

Department stores include House of Fraser stores, John Lewis stores, Allders stores. Usually in city centres, they are attractively laid out stores selling all kinds of goods. The staff are usually well informed about the goods they sell. They offer an after-sales service and various kinds of credit accounts.

Multiple stores You see the same branches in most shopping centres in the country, such as Saxone, Mothercare, W.H. Smith, Dewhurst. They specialize in one particular kind of goods and have a similar range and quality, no matter which town or city the branch is in.

Discount centres, for example, Comet or Argos. They print newspapers or catalogues listing the goods offered for sale and their prices, which are usually low. In the store you can look at a sample on display. If you decide to buy, you fill in the details on a form and hand it in. The item is brought out from a warehouse behind the showroom. Their advantages are the low prices and the wide variety of goods offered. They offer money-back guarantees if you are not happy with the goods for any reason when you get them home and unpack them. They may offer an after-sales service for repairs.

Bar coding

Many of the products we buy from supermarkets or large stores have a square of numbered black lines of varying thickness on the wrapping. The square is called a 'bar code' and is part of an electronic system increasingly being used in shops.

Each group of lines of the bar code gives certain information. The first two reveal the country the product has come from, the next five reveal the manufacturer of the product, the next five identify the product itself. The thirteenth group is an accuracy check.

As you take your purchases out of your basket at the checkout the assistant will pass the code on each product through a laser scan. The laser unit is linked to a computer which holds the price of each item. The price is retrieved from the computer file, displayed on the till for the customer to see, and both the name of the product and its price are printed on the receipt. This means that it is easy to check exactly what you have bought and what it has cost, when you get home. At the same time the computer records the sale of each item so that the shop knows at any time how much of any product has been sold and how much is in stock.

Shopping for food

Supermarkets are mainly for food although they often sell a few other household goods. They are self-service, usually cheaper than smaller food shops, sell most foods under one roof, and offer a wide range to choose from. They often stay open late several evenings a week.

Specialist food shops sell one particular type of food, and include butchers, bakers, and greengrocers. They are usually very good because they concentrate on one type of food only. The quality of the food is usually high, they often have a wider range to choose from than the supermarket and offer a more personal service to the customers.

Corner shops are situated much closer to where people live, so they are very convenient for quick shopping. They are often 'open all hours' and sell as wide a variety of goods as they can fit into the space available. Their prices are higher than in supermarkets because they do not have as high a turnover, but they do offer personal service. You can call in and out much more quickly than you can in a supermarket, especially if you only want a couple of items.

Markets are good for really fresh food, particularly fruit and vegetables, at the lowest possible prices. They can keep prices low because they do not have high bills to pay for rent, heat, light, and so on.

Questions

1 **What are the advantages of shopping at hypermarkets?**
2 **Why is shopping at Discount Centres popular?**
3 **What are the advantages of department stores for shopping?**
4 **What is a 'bar code'? How is it useful to (a) the customer and (b) the shop?**
5 **What benefits can a local corner shop offer even though prices may be higher?**
6 **Name six 'speciality shops' found in most high streets or shopping centres.**

Making consumer decisions

When you decide that you want to buy goods that are to last for a long time, it pays you to look around carefully before you part with your money. If you rush out and buy the first item you see you may soon find that it is not after all exactly what you wanted, or that you could have bought it more cheaply in another shop. Once you have decided that you want a certain item, perhaps a computer, a bedroom carpet, or a portable television, you have to work out what you can afford to spend. Then there are three other considerations you ought to think about:

1 Where you can get information about what you want.
2 Which particular type or model you want.
3 Deciding where to buy it.

Information about what you want

To help you in your choice, you can get information from several sources, including:

a Consumer Advice Centres (run by local councils) can give you details. (See page 162.)
b Books like this one, and magazines like *Good Housekeeping*, give advice on what to look for when you choose. In this book, for example, there is advice on choosing refrigerators on page 114, carpets on page 83, washing machines on page 128. Sometimes a magazine will describe and compare individual models which are on sale at the time.
c *Which?* magazine (see page 162) describes particular models you may be considering. The library will help you find the copy you want.
d Shops selling the goods will be able to give you advice.
e Quite a lot of general information can be had from radio and television consumer programmes, from friends, newspapers, and advertisements.

Choosing the type or model you want

Once you have decided in general what you want to buy you need to know something about the different models you might be considering. You will want to know:

a What is available at the price you can afford.
b The design features you want.
c Whether it has a useful guarantee. (See page 161.) If so, for how long?
d Whether it is likely to need much after-sale servicing. What are the arrangements for this?
e What size you will need. For example, if it is a refrigerator, will it fit into the space available, and is it large enough for your family?

Deciding where to buy

You could buy from a department store, discount centre such as Comet, electricity or gas showroom, Argos catalogue centre, electrical shop, hypermarket, or by mail order. Where you finally buy will be affected by:

a What is available where you live.

b The price – several shops and discount centres have a policy of refunding any difference to you if you can buy more cheaply elsewhere what you have bought from them.

c Whether credit facilities are offered if you want them. If so, you need to know the A.P.R. and how it will affect the price.

d Servicing – do they offer an after-sales service? Sometimes a small electrical shop has a good reputation for this and you could consider whether it is worth paying a little extra on the price for this service.

e Whether the goods are in stock or whether you will have to wait.

f Delivery – is this available, and if so, is there a charge for it?

Questions

1 **Why could you regret having bought goods in a hurry?**

2 **If you were thinking of buying a radio/cassette player, which three sources of information would you be most likely to use?**

3 **Price is a very important consideration when choosing most consumer goods. What other points are also important?**

4 **What kinds of goods do you think are most likely to need after-sales service?**

5 **Why is it useful to shop at a store where staff have specialist knowledge?**

Further work on chapter 7

1   Your mother has agreed to buy you a radio/cassette player for your birthday, paying for it in instalments. Choose the one you would like, then collect the necessary information for your mother about paying for it.

2   You want to start saving from your Saturday job to pay for a holiday next year. Look around in the area where you live and decide on the most suitable place to open an account.

3   Your brother/sister wants to buy an inexpensive second-hand car but does not want to be taken for a ride! What can he/she do to find out his/her rights before buying?

4   You want to open a credit account with a local shop or department store to help you spread the cost of buying clothes. How would you decide which store to select?

5   Your mother wants to buy a washing-machine and has decided on the model she wants. It is on sale in three different local shops and in her mail order catalogue. How should she decide where to buy it?

Sources of further information

Banking Information Service, 10 Lombard St., London EC3V 9AT have a catalogue of films, videos, and booklets on money management and banking.

Office of Fair Trading, Room 310C, Field House, Bream's Building, London EC4A 1PR has many leaflets on consumer affairs, shopping problems, etc. These are often available at Consumer Advice Centres and Citizens' Advice Bureaux.

Films
CFL Vision, 237 Chalfont Grove, Gerrards Cross, Bucks., SL9 8TN has a catalogue of many films and videos on money and consumer affairs.

EFVA (address on page 52) also has many films on these subjects.

Books
Consumer Education by Ian Cooper, Oxford University Press.
Things You Need To Know by Pen Keyte, Oxford University Press.

Chapter 8

Looking after the family

The expectant mother

Diet

An unborn baby relies completely upon his mother to supply the foods he needs. He will take from her the nutrients he needs for his own body to develop and grow soundly, so she should have some knowledge of which foods are needed for this.

The mother does not need to 'eat for two' in the sense of eating twice the quantity but she does need extra foods rich in the nutrients needed for her baby to develop well and to keep herself in good health.

Extra foods

Protein. A good intake of protein foods is needed. The baby's bones, muscles, tissues and so on all contain protein. If they are to grow and develop fully he needs a good supply of protein which he can only get from his mother. An extra pint of milk daily will meet her extra need, or an increased intake of meat, cheese, fish, yoghurt, nuts or other protein-rich foods.

Calcium is the essential part of both the bones and teeth. If the baby is to have a strong, well-formed bone structure, then a good supply of calcium is essential. A daily pint of milk, and cheese, will provide what is needed.

Vitamin D (Cholecalciferol) is sometimes called the calcifying vitamin, because it is needed before the body can actually make use of calcium for the bone structure. It is found in butter, margarine, and oily fish, and is also produced by the action of sunlight on the skin.

Vitamin C (Ascorbic acid) is needed for the baby's normal growth, for protection against infection and to help the body absorb iron. You need a good supply of this each day, as the body does not store it. It is found in raw fruit and vegetables and in special fruit drinks (blackcurrant, rose-hip or orange), labelled as having a high Vitamin C content. Ordinary fruit squashes normally contain very little.

Iron is very important during pregnancy for the production of sound red blood cells. For the first three or four months of his life the baby is fed only on milk which contains very little iron. He is born with a store of iron in his liver which lasts him during this time. He will take the iron he needs from his mother before he is born. If she does not have enough iron for the needs of the baby and herself she may become anaemic, tire easily, and be weak and breathless. Plenty of iron-rich foods will avoid this – liver, kidney, red meats, corned beef, egg yolk, black pudding, dried fruit, black treacle and cocoa.

The other vitamins and minerals too are important for the proper growth and development of your child. There will normally be an adequate supply of these from a good varied diet. Try to include the following foods in your diet:

1 – 1½ pints of milk daily
Liver weekly
Oily fish weekly
Meat, cheese, eggs, yoghurt
Fresh fruit and vegetables
Cereals and wholegrain bread

Foods to avoid

Too many rich, fried, fatty or sugary foods are not good for anyone. They can make you put on too much weight and may aggravate any sickness, indigestion or heartburn you may have during pregnancy. Strong tea or coffee sometimes has the same effect, as does highly spiced or seasoned food. You may find that foods you normally like do not agree with you any more.

Smoking can do positive damage to your baby's health. It is well worth trying to stop or cut down and to avoid places with a very smoky atmosphere.

Alcohol should only be drunk in moderation. Remember that alcohol is a drug and can affect your baby. It is better to avoid spirits like whisky and gin.

Extra vitamin or iron tablets may be prescribed for you by your doctor, but you should not take them or any other medicines or tablets such as aspirins, sickness pills or laxatives without first asking medical advice, as they could affect the developing baby.

Dental care during pregnancy

The baby will draw the calcium for forming his own bones and teeth from his mother, so you need a good supply. You should:
a Eat plenty of foods rich in calcium – milk, cheese, white flour.
b Visit your dentist often. Treatment is free for expectant mothers and until the baby is a year old.
c Take extra care with cleaning your teeth. You should clean after breakfast, then after every meal if possible, and never go to bed without cleaning your teeth first.

Care of hair and skin

Keep your hair in an easily managed, easily washed style. It may become more or less greasy than usual. Your skin will often improve, especially if you take particular care about your diet.

Ante-natal care

If you miss one period you may wonder whether you are pregnant. If you miss two it is quite possible that you are, and a visit to your doctor will enable you to find out whether you are or not. If you are pregnant, the doctor will usually send you to a local clinic for ante-natal care.

The ante-natal clinic provides the following services:
1 Regular medical checks are made to make sure you keep in good health.
2 Your weight gain is checked. It should not normally be more than 24–28 lbs. altogether.
3 Advice is given on any problems you may have – perhaps about diet, hygiene, preparing for breast feeding, or arranging home help.
4 Mothercraft classes are often run by local clinics, with friendly and informal advice on how to choose your baby's clothes and nursery equipment, how to feed, bath and look after him or her.
5 Relaxation classes will teach you exercises and ways of relaxing your body which help you while the baby is being born.

6   At the clinic you will meet other expectant mothers. This gives you an opportunity to make friends and to discuss the interests and problems you may have in common.

Post-natal care

After the birth of the baby you can go to a clinic for post-natal care. Here are some of the ways in which they can give you help and advice:

1   They will check your health and give you advice on how to regain your muscle tone by exercising.
2   Your baby's health and weight gain will be checked.
3   Vaccination for your baby will be discussed and arranged.
4   The clinic will give help and support on any problems you may have, perhaps with feeding your baby or with caring for him in any way.
5   They will discuss and advise you on family planning so that you can have the number of children you would like, and can look after, when you want them.
6   They often sell welfare foods, such as dried milk and vitamin foods.
7   Again, you meet other mothers of young babies with whom you can talk and make friends.

The midwife is concerned with the health of the mother and the baby up to two weeks old. Whether the baby is born in hospital or at home she comes to visit you at home daily until two weeks after the birth.

The health visitor is concerned with the baby from the age of two weeks to five years. She is a trained nurse, midwife and health visitor and will visit you at home to advise and help with the care of the baby or with coping with everyday family problems.

Home helps can be arranged through your doctor or clinic, to come and help at home with all the jobs a mother normally does – cooking, shopping, cleaning, washing – until the mother is fit enough to do them herself. You pay for this service according to how much you can afford.

Financial help

Free or cheap milk and welfare foods are available to many expectant mothers and their young children. The clinic will advise you about this.

The maternity grant must be applied for to the Social Fund. (See page 186.) If you have a low income you can apply to the fund for a loan which must usually be repaid by deduction from your weekly social security payments.

Maternity Allowance is a weekly allowance paid to those mothers who have been employed and paying full National Insurance contributions. It is paid for eleven weeks before the baby is due and seven weeks afterwards, provided the mother does not work at this time. It enables her to give up working in good time before the birth of the baby so that she can keep herself fit and rested, and it means that she does not need to return to work too soon afterwards.

Child benefit is a sum paid weekly, usually to the mother, for all the children in the family, including the first. It was formerly called the Family Allowance. An extra allowance is paid to one-parent families.

Single mothers are entitled to the same help and benefits. They often need extra help and support, and their doctor or clinic will always put them in touch with an organization sympathetic and willing to help.

'Lifeline' is just one of the voluntary bodies who give free and practical help of many kinds, including help with housing, work and possible adoption, to anyone facing an unwanted pregnancy, whether married or not.

Questions

1 **Which nutrients should an expectant mother take extra care to include in her diet?**
2 **Name three foods which will give a good supply of each one of these.**
3 **Name some foods it might be better to avoid during pregnancy.**
4 **Is it a good idea for an expectant mother to smoke and drink a lot? Why?**
5 **How would you take particular care of your teeth during pregnancy?**
6 **How can (a) ante-natal and (b) post-natal clinics help a mother and baby?**
7 **Describe the financial help an expectant mother could expect to receive.**

Baby care

Caring for her first baby can be a very enjoyable time for a new mother, but at the same time she may often feel anxious about many aspects of looking after him or her and may wonder whether she is doing the 'right' thing. In this country a mother can find help and advice easily, not only from her family and friends but from her doctor, midwife, clinic or health visitor.

Feeding

Breast-feeding
Whenever possible, a baby should be breast-fed, because:

1. Breast milk contains exactly what is required for the baby's needs.
2. It is always clean, fresh and at the right temperature.
3. It contains substances which help the baby resist infection.
4. It costs nothing and is readily available.
5. It does not involve preparing feeds or sterilizing bottles.
6. It helps the development of a close and affectionate relationship between mother and baby.

Bottle-feeding
This may sometimes be necessary, in which case the baby is fed on cow's milk, either dried, fresh or evaporated. It is extremely important to follow exactly the advice of your doctor or clinic about the quantities the baby needs, and the correct preparation of feeds.

Bottle-feeding does have these advantages:

1. It means a baby can be fed even if his mother cannot feed him.
2. Someone else can feed the baby if the mother is not available.
3. You can see exactly how much milk the child is getting.

A bottle-fed baby should always be held closely and affectionately by his mother, so that he feels as secure and loved as a breast-fed baby would do.

Cleanliness

Everything concerned with a baby's milk must be absolutely clean. Harmful bacteria will quickly grow in milk and could cause serious illness. Your hands and everything you use should be well washed before you prepare a bottle. Bottles and teats must be sterilized after use.

Sterilizing bottles

This can be done by (a) rinsing, washing, then boiling bottles and teats for the correct length of time, or (b) rinsing, washing, then soaking bottles and teats in a special hypochlorite solution (the 'Milton' method). Whichever method you use it is essential to get detailed instructions from your clinic and to follow them exactly.

Extra vitamin-rich foods

Your clinic or doctor will advise you as to exactly when and how to introduce these foods to give your baby the best possible start. From the age of a few weeks, he may need extra nutrients which are not available in breast milk and cow's milk.

Vitamin C can be provided by special fruit juice or syrup, usually orange or rose-hip.
Vitamins A and D are usually supplied by drops of a cod-liver oil preparation.
Iron can be provided by sieved egg yolk.

These vitamins, foods and also dried milk are usually sold at your local clinic or chemist.

Weaning

This means introducing solid foods to a baby who has only been used to milk. Weaning is a gradual process during which you should aim to get him or her used to a varied diet, beginning with finely mashed or sieved foods. He may not like the feeling of a spoon and food in his mouth at first as he has only been used to sucking, so it is best to give him just a little solid food to taste at the beginning of a feed when he is still hungry enough to try it.

Questions

1   **Suggest five ways in which a mother could find help or advice if she had any problems in caring for her small child.**
2   **What do you think are the four most important reasons for breast-feeding a baby?**
3   **Why do you think some mothers do not breast-feed their babies?**
4   **Why is extra care about cleanliness needed when preparing babies' bottles?**
5   **Briefly describe two possible ways of sterilizing bottles and teats. Which method would you advise a mother to use and why?**
6   **What are the reasons why babies should never be left alone to feed themselves from a bottle?**
7   **Name four nutrients needed by a growing baby which milk does not supply. Say how you would provide your baby with each one.**
8   **Describe how you would start to wean your baby on to solid food.**

Clothes for a baby

Clothes for a young baby should be soft, warm and light, made of absorbent material, easy to put on and take off and easy to wash and iron. Do not be tempted to buy too many of the first size as the baby will very quickly grow out of them.

The layette

A layette means the clothes you collect in preparation for an expected baby. It will include most of the articles listed below, and will depend partly on the time of year the baby is born.

Nappies – at least two dozen.

Vests These should be either pure wool or cotton, depending on the time of year. They should be easy to put on and take off without pulling. Either an 'envelope-stye' neck or a front-opening type fastened with ribbon is best.

Stretch-towelling suits are ideal for wear during the day or night. They cover the baby from below his head to his toes and leave no gaps. They can be easily machine-washed and do not need ironing. They stretch a little as the baby grows and so last quite well, though of course they should not be allowed to become too tight.

Nightgowns may be worn instead of stretch suits. They are often made of winceyette (brushed cotton) which is a highly inflammable material. This means they are only suitable for a small baby who is too young to crawl around. (See page 181.)

Matinee jackets are light, knitted cardigans, used for extra warmth whenever needed.

Hats, bootees and mittens for cooler weather. You can also buy smooth mittens which help to stop babies scratching their faces.

Shawl or soft blanket A small baby likes to be firmly wrapped up at first. A knitted or cellular small blanket or shawl is ideal.

Bibs, usually made of towelling, protect a baby's clothes during a feed. They may be plastic-backed, and for safety must be taken off after the feed.

Nappies

There are many different types of nappies available. By trying different kinds a mother can find out what suits her and her baby best.

1 *Towelling nappies* are soft and absorbent. You will need a couple of dozen at least.

2 *Muslin nappies* are thinner and lighter. They may be used instead of towelling nappies for a very small baby or in hot weather.

3 *Disposable nappies,* worn inside plastic pants, are thick and soft. They save you having to wash nappies but it can be rather expensive to use them all the time. It is better to burn them than to flush them away, as they are quite a frequent cause of blocked drains.

4   *Nappy liners* are like strong paper handkerchiefs worn inside a towelling nappy. They will hold any soiling and can be flushed away easily so that the outer nappy is easier to wash.

5   *One-way nappies,* made of soft material, are worn inside a towelling nappy. The moisure passes through to the outer nappy and the side next to the baby's skin stays dry, cutting down the risk of nappy rash.

Washing

Babies' skin is particularly sensitive, so only a mild detergent should be used for their clothes. Rinsing should be thorough. The use of a fabric conditioner will keep the clothes soft.

Nappies should be soaked and washed in very hot water or boiled. This will keep them white and kill any germs which could cause nappy rash. Rinse them well and dry them out of doors or in a tumble-drier to keep them soft.

Instead of washing, nappies may be soaked in a solution of sanitizing powder. This will whiten them and kill any bacteria. Rinse them well in cold water afterwards and dry as usual.

Equipment

Look for the following points when choosing equipment for your baby.

Pram – good brakes, waterproof mattress, will not tip easily, collapsible if you want to take it in a car, fittings for a safety harness, comfortable to push.

Cot – firm, waterproof mattress, lead-free paint, bars not too far apart, strongly made, a drop-side with a firm catch. Look for the Kitemark.

Bath and stand – make sure they are firm and steady.

High or Low Chair – steady, easy to clean, fitting for a safety harness.

Nursing chair – with low legs so the baby will not easily roll off your lap.

Toiletries

Many toiletries are specially made for babies' delicate skins. They include baby lotion and oil for cleaning, creams to protect the skin from nappy rash, talcum power, mild soap and shampoo, cotton wool and cotton buds.

Questions

1   **When choosing any clothes for a small baby, what qualities would you look for?**

2   **What clothes are included in a layette? Say what you would look for when choosing each one.**

3   **Describe the different kinds of nappies you can buy, giving the advantages and disadvantages of each kind.**

4   **What general rules would you follow when washing clothes for a baby?**

5   **You are helping a friend choose a pram, cot and baby bath and stand. What safety features would you advise her to look for, for each item?**

The safety of children

Vaccination

Vaccines are available to protect children from several serious infections, including poliomyelitis (polio), diphtheria, tetanus and whooping cough, all of which were once common causes of serious illness and death.

It is important for parents to know what vaccines are available for preventing disease in their children and to know both the benefits and the possible risks.

Polio

Polio often causes permanent paralysis and in some cases death. The general use of vaccination has nearly eliminated the disease, but when this happens and parents feel it is not worth vaccinating their children, there can be a sudden increase in the number of cases of polio in unvaccinated children. Polio vaccine very seldom has any harmful effects. Only rarely – once in more than a million cases – has a person who has received the vaccine developed paralysis.

Diphtheria/Tetanus/Whooping Cough – Triple Vaccine

Vaccination against these three diseases may be combined in one vaccine which gives protection against all three, though they can all be given separately if it should be wished.

Diphtheria

This is a very serious infection of the nose and throat. National vaccination has reduced the number of cases from 50 000 a year to less than 10 in 1977.

Tetanus

This results from infected wounds or cuts which may appear only slight in themselves. It is a severe disease and can kill, but it can be prevented by vaccination.

Whooping cough

This is a highly infectious and distressing chest infection which can damage the lungs. Babies can suffer seriously from it and may die.

Following evidence that whooping cough vaccine has, in a very small number of cases resulted in a serious reaction affecting the brain and nervous system, it has become less of a routine vaccination. The decision, of course, rests finally with the parents. Unfortunately, though, this reduced number of children receiving vaccinations has led to a sharp increase in the number of whooping-cough cases reported, from 4000 in 1976 to over 17 000 in 1977.

It is important for parents to realize that when they decide which diseases to have their children vaccinated against, they should base their decision on a careful study of the facts and figures available, and they should discuss their own particular case with their doctor or health visitor. There is no doubt at all that vaccination has very effectively reduced the likelihood of a child developing a serious disease and the risk of any serious reaction from the vaccination itself is very uncommon.

Doubts about the whooping-cough vaccine should not deter parents from having the other vaccinations available to their children. A 'scare' that vaccination is likely to cause serious illness may make parents decide against vaccination, but when this happens the number of cases of the disease increases, so that unvaccinated children are then more likely to develop the infection as a result.

Your local clinic will start a suitable programme of vaccination in babyhood and this will be completed when the child goes to school. A careful record should be kept of which vaccinations were given and when, as it is easy to forget details when the programme is spread over a number of years.

Safety rules when looking after babies

1 Do not use a pillow for young babies – it is not necessary. A firm, flat safety pillow is the only safe kind if you must use one at all.
2 Tuck babies in firmly, so that blankets cannot cover the face.
3 Put a baby to sleep on his side rather than his back, so that if he brings up a little feed he will not choke on it.
4 A baby should not sleep with adults or older children, because of the danger of smothering.
5 Do not use plastic sheets or covers in cots or prams, as this could lead to suffocation.
6 Never leave a baby alone with a plastic bib on.
7 Never leave a baby alone to suck from a bottle, as he could easily choke.
8 Use a safety net to keep cats from sleeping on the baby when he is out in his pram. The cat may be attracted by the warmth.
9 As soon as a baby can sit up make sure he is securely harnessed into his pram or high chair, which should be steady.
10 Keep small buttons, beads or toys away from a baby, as he will automatically put them in his mouth.

The safety of young children

Many serious accidents happen at home every year. Children under five have a particularly high number of accidents, as you can see from these figures for one particular year.

Cause of accident	Age 0–4 years	Age 5–14 years
Suffocation/choking	664	11
Poisoning	71	17
Falls	66	11

Suffocation and choking

Suffocation and choking cause death as the child is unable to breathe. Follow all the rules given above when looking after small babies. Once babies start to walk and explore there are more dangers to avoid:

1 A few inches of water can drown a small child. Never leave him alone to play in the bath or near a shallow pool or stream.
2 Keep all polythene bags out of the reach of children.
3 An old refrigerator should have the door removed before being thrown away, as a small child could get trapped inside.
4 Cut food into small pieces. Remove bones, eggshell, tough meat, and stringy vegetables.

Poisoning

1 Keep all pills, medicines and tablets right out of a child's reach. Remember that a determined child will climb up on chairs or tables. A cupboard with a lock is best. 'Child-proof' bottle tops have proved to be much safer than ordinary ones.
2 Keep household cleaners out of the reach of the toddler. Many are highly poisonous. Bleach, disinfectant, polishes, cleansing liquids and powders, and turpentine are within easy reach of a curious child in many households, often under the sink.
3 Garden sprays, weedkillers, paints, paraffin and so on should be out of reach in a garage or shed. All of these could kill if swallowed.
4 Never put chemicals, cleaners or anything else into an empty squash or lemonade bottle. A child could drink it, thinking it was lemonade.
5 Some common garden plants are poisonous. These include rhubarb leaves, privet, laburnum seeds, holly and other berries. Teach children not to eat things picked up in the garden.
6 Town gas is poisonous. Do not leave a child alone where he could turn on a gas tap.
7 Always use lead-free paint for anything a child might chew – cots and toys especially. Lead is poisonous and can cause brain damage.

Falls

1 Have a firm safety gate at the top and bottom of the stairs.
2 Try to avoid leaving toys around the floor.
3 Do not have highly polished floors or loose mats. Mop up spills straight away.
4 Take care with open windows and balconies. Do not leave chairs near them which children could use to climb on.
5 Do not leave small children on a table even for a few seconds.
6 A cot should have the B.S.I. Kitemark. The fastening should be strong and the sides should be high enough.
7 Loose, poorly-fitting shoes can cause a fall.
8 Prams and high chairs should be steady, with a fitting for a safety harness.

Scalds and burns
1 Unguarded fires are dangerous and illegal. Take extra care with portable fires.
2 Keep matches away from children.
3 Do not let pan handles stick out over the edge of a cooker.
4 Avoid tablecloths hanging down over the edge of the table where they could be pulled. Keep hot tea-pots away from the edge of the table.
5 Test bath water before putting a child in.
6 Take care when drinking or carrying hot liquids such as tea or coffee.
7 Flame-proof material should be used for clothes where possible. All nighties and frilly party dresses for children must, by law, be made of flame-proof material. This should be carefully washed to keep its finish. Avoid buying winceyette (brushed cotton) for making children's nightdresses. It is highly inflammable and should never be used for this purpose.

Road safety
Train your child from the beginning in road safety, and always set a good example yourself. Do not leave children to play in a garden where they could run on to the road.

Child safety in cars
Under the law which came into effect in January 1983, it is the responsibility of the driver to ensure that any child under 14 in the front seat of a car wears a seat belt or restraint. Any child over the age of one can wear any approved child restraint or seat belt. A child under one must be in an approved restraint designed for a child of that age or size. All adults and children over 14 are responsible themselves for wearing a seat belt.

Although the law insists only on seat belts for the front of the car as it is the most dangerous place, responsible parents can make their child safer by fitting a child safety seat, harness, seat belt or carry cot straps.

Questions
1 **Name four illnesses which can be prevented by vaccination.**
2 **What points would you as a parent consider when deciding about vaccinations for your child?**
3 **Where can you get information on the different vaccines available?**
4 **How would you usually know when your child was due for a vaccination?**
5 **Why do you think young babies are particularly likely to suffocate?**
6 **What points would you be especially careful about when putting a baby to sleep in a cot or pram?**
7 **What precautions can you take to avoid a small child suffocating or choking?**
8 **Your three-year-old cousin is coming to stay with your family for a few days. Describe the precautions you would take around the house to prevent the possibility of the child being poisoned.**
9 **Name some of the most common causes of accidental falls in the home.**
10 **What precautions can you take to avoid scalds and burns?**

Children under school age

Children have many needs which have to be met if they are to grow into happy, healthy adults. For pre-school children, all these needs should be met either at home or in pre-school nursery groups of various kinds.

Physical care
Physical care is the most obvious need. Children have to be properly fed and kept clean and warm. They need suitable activity to become physically well developed and healthy. A good nursery will provide well-chosen equipment in an area specially planned to suit the children.

Emotional and social development
Children have to learn to cope with their feelings about themselves and about other people. The first feelings of a small baby will all centre on himself, then he gradually extends his feelings to his mother, then his closest family and slowly he becomes sufficiently self-confident to be able to cope with a larger group outside his own family circle. A good nursery class or group can encourage this development at a rate the child can manage, by widening the circle of adults and other children he mixes with.

A child's emotional development affects the whole of his personality. Patterns can be set up in the first few years of his life which affect both the way he gets on with other people and his ability to learn and generally manage for the rest of his life.

Intellectual development
The first five years or so of a child's life are vital in the development of his intelligence. This is important not only to his educational future but to his ability to grow into an independent, thinking adult.

The child should be provided with a variety of stimulating activities and experiences which will encourage him to think for himself, to work things out and to explore and understand his environment. He should be encouraged to use words and language so that he can learn to organize and express his thoughts.

Why day-care for pre-school children is needed

Until quite recently it was accepted as normal that nearly all mothers who had children should stay at home to look after them. As long as the mother wants to do this and is able to provide a warm, affectionate and interesting family life, this is probably the best background a child can have, particularly in the first few years of his life.

However, there are many reasons why this is not always possible and the role of women is changing because of them.

1   Many women want to go out to work. They enjoy the companionship and independence this gives them. This does not mean that they do not want children but rather that they want children *and* a job, so that care for their children under school age is needed.

2   Most families are now limited in size so that by the time a woman is in her late twenties or early thirties she may have had all the children she plans to have, and so is less tied to her home.

3   Housework takes less time than it did with the widespread use of convenience foods, washing machines, vacuum cleaners, refrigerators, freezers and so on. This means women have more time to spare.

4   The cost of living – including housing, fuel, food and clothing – may be so high that a family may need the extra income from the mother's job to provide an acceptable standard of living.

5   Many families used to live in close-knit communities, with grandmothers, aunts and other relations living nearby, who were easily available to help with the care of the children. These communities are now breaking up and families may now have no close relatives living nearby to help.

6   There are cases of special need, for example, an unsupported mother, an unfortunate background of poor or overcrowded housing conditions, ill-health, mental or physical handicap, or a general inability to cope with looking after children. In such cases it is desirable to provide help for families with caring for their children.

Questions

1   **Describe briefly the kind of care children need if they are to be physically well developed and healthy.**

2   **What stages does a small child pass through as he learns to mix socially? How can a good nursery group help in this development?**

3   **Why is it important to help a young child to develop emotionally?**

4   **In what ways could you encourage the development of a small child's intelligence?**

5   **Why do you think many mothers want to go out to work, even if they do not really need the money?**

6   **In what circumstances do you think mothers really need help in caring for their children?**

7   **If you had two children under five, and enough money, would you want to go out to work? Give all the reasons you can think of.**

8   **Do you think your children would develop better in all ways if you were at home or at work?**

Facilities for pre-school children

Private day nurseries

These are often good but are usually rather expensive and so are most frequently used by parents who are better off. They have to be registered with the local authority who make checks on safety, numbers, staff, hygiene facilities and so on. Many thousands of children attend these private nurseries. Sometimes they are attached to factories or colleges and are only for the use of those parents working there. They usually cater only for children over two or three years old, and much less frequently for babies.

Pre-school play groups

These also have to be registered with the local authority. They are normally run by some of the parents whose children attend the group and are often held in a church hall or community centre on perhaps two or three mornings or afternoons a week. They are only part-time and provide an opportunity for the child's social development through play with others, but of course they do not provide the full daily care of the child which is required by working parents and which is provided by a day nursery.

Local authority day nurseries

These are usually run by the Department of Health and Social Security and are primarily concerned with the physical care of the children in their charge, as compared with nursery classes or schools whose main concern is with educational development.

Children can attend these nurseries from the age of six weeks to five years old, and they are usually open from early in the morning until the evening, to cater for parents who have to work a full day.

There are long waiting lists for these nurseries and priority is given to parents who for social reasons must go out to work, for example a mother who has no husband to support her and the child. Other parents who are unable to cope with looking after their children themselves, perhaps because of poor housing or mental or physical inability to run a home and family, also have priority. This means that a mother who would like to work but does not have to do so for financial reasons often has very little chance of obtaining a place for her child in a local authority day nursery, though the number of places available varies a great deal from one area to another. There are usually more in inner city areas where there tends to be a higher number of families with greater social need.

Nursery classes, nursery units, nursery schools

These are run by the Department of Education and Science and are primarily concerned with encouraging intellectual development so that children have a good start when they begin compulsory schooling at five years old. They usually take children from three or four years old depending on the number of places available. Again priority is usually given to opening nursery classes in city areas, though some local authorities are trying to extend this to offer places to all who would like them.

Child minders

More children below school age are looked after by child minders than by any other scheme, though as these arrangements are usually privately made between individuals no exact figures are available. Child minders are encouraged to register with the local authority, so that checks can be made to cut down the possibilities of overcrowding, lack of facilities for playing, unsafe conditions and so on. Some authorities have encouraged child minders to register with them by operating a free lending service of toys, books, fireguards and other equipment and by offering help and advice.

Questions

1 **What are the advantages and disadvantages of private nurseries for parents who are out at work?**
2 **Describe how a pre-school play group is usually run.**
3 **Where would you expect to find most local authority day nurseries? Explain why.**
4 **Describe fully the services provided by a local authority day nursery.**
5 **What is the difference between a local authority day nursery and a nursery school or class?**
6 **You want to go out to work and are considering having your child looked after by a child minder. Make a list of all the points you would look for when deciding whether or not she would offer suitable care for your child.**

Social security benefits

The system of benefits for the sick, old, unemployed, disabled, and others was reorganized by the Social Security Act 1986, with most changes being brought in by April 1988. The cost of these benefits is met by various taxes and by National Insurance Contributions made by all employers and employees.

It is not always easy to work out whether or not you may be entitled to certain benefits. You can get information by:

a Asking at your local Department of Health and Social Security (D.H.S.S.) office.

b Reading leaflets published by the D.H.S.S. As amounts and figures change every year, make sure you have up-to-date leaflets.

c Most towns have a Citizen's Advice Bureau or Welfare Rights Office which will help you sort out any problems.

Who is entitled to benefits?

Some benefits are means-tested. That means you have to declare all the money you have (from any source) and if it is below a certain level you can receive the benefit.

Other benefits, like Child Benefit, you are entitled to no matter how high your income might be.

Some, like Unemployment Benefit and Retirement Pension, are contributary. That means you are only entitled to them if you have paid enough National Insurance contributions.

Some of the new benefits

Income Support If your income is below a certain level and you are not in full-time work you may receive Income Support. A certain amount is allowed for each adult and child. This is a means-tested benefit and replaces Supplementary Benefit.

Family Credit Paid to families where the breadwinner is working but the income is below a certain level. It replaces Family Income Supplement.

The Social Fund This is a fund to which people on low incomes can apply for a loan. The loan may be for maternity expenses, funeral expenses, special needs such as furniture, a cooker, or fuel debts. It is normally a loan, which must be paid off. In some instances this might be done by making weekly deductions from benefits.

Housing Benefit This is to help those on a low income to pay their rent and some of their rates.

Free school meals and milk Children in families receiving Income Support can receive free school meals and milk.

Other benefits

Child Benefit - payable for all children in the family, usually to the mother.

Unemployment Benefit – payable when people first become unemployed, provided that they have paid enough National Insurance contributions.

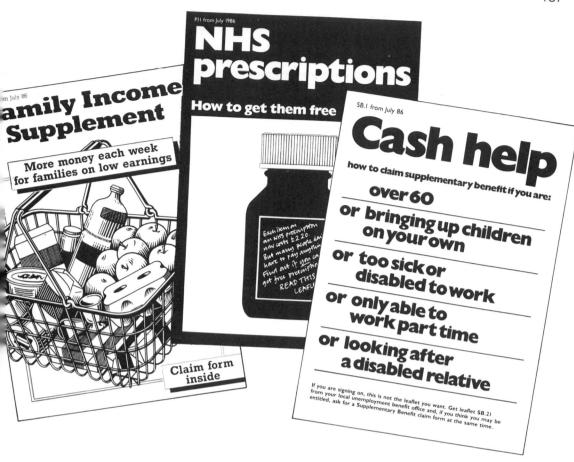

Sickness Benefit – if you are unable to work through illness. After some weeks you would be paid Invalidity Benefit instead.

Retirement Benefit – paid to those who have retired if they have made enough National Insurance contributions.

Widows Benefit – a lump sum at the time of bereavement and allowances for children up to 19.

Attendance Allowance – for those who are severely disabled mentally or physically and who need a lot of looking after.

Invalid Care Allowance – for people of working age who cannot go out to work because they have a severely disabled relative to care for.

Mobility Allowance – available as a cash benefit to help you to achieve mobility if you cannot work through physical disability. It is an alternative to an invalid vehicle for those who want it.

Questions

1 **You are uncertain as to whether or not you qualify for certain welfare benefits. How would you obtain exact information about this?**
2 **Where does the money come from to pay for social security benefits?**
3 **Who is entitled to Family Credit?**
4 **What is meant by a means-tested benefit?**

Help for handicapped people

There are many different kinds of services and cash benefits available to handicapped people, both through state schemes and through voluntary organizations. The Social Services department of the local authority usually has information about the help that is available from all sources and can advise you on your particular needs and how they can be met.

Financial help

Some of the benefits described on pages 186–7 may be available to handicapped people. These include invalidity benefits, industrial injury and disablement benefits, attendance allowance, invalid car allowance and mobility allowance.

Health services

The services of doctors and hospitals are provided free under the National Health Service. This may include all the cost of a long or short stay in a suitable hospital. Sometimes a short stay in hospital can be arranged to relieve the relatives of a handicapped person for a week or two. Help with transport to and from hospital can be provided.

Help with rehabilitation is given while you are in hospital to enable you to become as independent as possible. This could include physiotherapy, which involves exercises and treatment, and occupational therapy, which teaches you how you can carry out the usual activities of washing, dressing, cooking and following your normal interests, perhaps with the help of special equipment. Speech therapy helps those whose speech has suffered through illness or disability.

Social Services

This department of the local authority can help you cope with any kind of problem arising in the family which is caused by illness or handicap. They may help with home helps, Meals-on-Wheels, laundry, installing and paying the rent of a telephone, or providing a radio, television or books. They may also provide various aids and equipment, such as specially adapted furniture, cutlery, plates and cups and equipment designed to help with reading, writing, housework, caring for children, and gardening.

Day centres
These are provided by some local authorities and enable the handicapped to take part in various activities. These may include light employment or educational handicrafts, or they may be purely social.

Day care
Day care can be provided for children under school age of handicapped parents or for children with a handicap, perhaps at a nursery, playgroup or with a registered child minder.

Holidays and recreation
Facilities for sport, outings, and social clubs may be available.

Voluntary organizations

The Social Services department can put you in touch with the voluntary organizations in your area who also provide help and services of various kinds, often working in co-operation with local authorities. They too, may lend or give equipment, and help with transport, outings, housing and social activities, or they may help with the daily tasks of changing library books, collecting pensions, doing shopping or lighting fires.

Cheap travel
In some areas, reduced cost travel is available on buses and trains.

Car badges
The disabled can obtain car badges which allow them to park where it would normally be restricted and to ignore the usual time limits.

Guides for touring
Some local authorities and the A.A. produce guides with information about hotels, restaurants and places to visit in the area which make provision for the needs of handicapped people.

Employment services
Assistance is available in looking for suitable employment and possible training courses.

Housing

Financial help may be provided for adapting a council house or a privately owned house for a handicapped person. Adaptations might include moving electrical switches and sockets, or providing handrails for a bath or toilet, a downstairs toilet, an easy-to-manage heating system, wider doors and ramps for a wheelchair. Some housing is specially designed and built for those people dependent on a wheelchair. Voluntary organizations, too, may provide housing.

Page 29 explains how gas and electrical appliances can be adapted for easier use by disabled people.

Handicapped children

Parents are given advice on the most suitable kind of education available, either in an ordinary school or in a special school if the handicap is severe. Home tuition is available for children who cannot go to school.

Questions

1 **Where would you go for information on the help available to handicapped people?**
2 **List some of the cash benefits which may be available.**
3 **What kind of help can the handicapped receive in hospital?**
4 **Describe the different provisions made by the Social Services department for the handicapped under these headings:**
   a In the home.
   b Outside the home.
5 **What kind of services are provided by voluntary organizations?**

The care of the elderly

Diet

Elderly people often have a rather poor diet, which can cause a general feeling of poor health, if not actual illness. This can be due to:

1   Shortage of money.
2   Lack of knowledge about which foods will keep them feeling well.
3   Poor teeth, or dentures which do not fit well.
4   Illness, handicap, or feeling unfit, which may cause difficulty in shopping.
5   Loneliness, which may cause them to feel it is not worth taking much trouble, especially if they are just cooking for one.
6   Poor cooking facilities. They may not have a refrigerator.

All these factors may result in a diet of foods which are easy to prepare and clear away and involve little cooking. Such foods are often starchy – bread, cakes, biscuits – and the diet will be deficient in the protein, minerals and vitamins needed for health. The diet should be well balanced and should include sufficient:

Protein – easiest to digest in the form of fish, poultry, eggs and milk.
Vitamin C – this is good for the gums and helps in the absorption of iron. It is easily provided by fruit juice or syrup, tomatoes and green vegetables.
Vitamin D and Calcium – lack of these can cause a curved spine and brittle bones. They are easily provided by milk and other dairy foods.
Iron – lack of this can cause fatigue from lack of oxygen. It can be provided by egg yolk, liver, corned beef, red meat, dried fruit and cocoa.

Safety

Many accidents happen to older people in their own homes, often because of poor sight, hearing or sense of balance and slower reactions. To help prevent accidents, take care to observe these general rules:

1   Good lighting is important around the house, with a bedside light for the night.
2   Floor coverings should be secure, with no loose mats or highly polished floors.
3   Firm, comfortable shoes and slippers should be worn.
4   Keep objects off the floor as far as possible. Avoid trailing flexes.
5   Have a good handrail on the stairs.
6   Use a non-slip mat in the bath and handles beside the bath, to help elderly people to get in and out of the bath safely.
7   Avoid heaters which can be knocked over. Have heaters serviced regularly.
8   Use hot water bottles with care. Use them with covers.
9   Electric blankets should have the B.S.I. Kitemark and be regularly serviced.
10   It is a good idea if in the morning old people put out any pills or medicines they need for that day, so that they remember to take them, but don't take them twice.

Housing

Housing will preferably be easy to run, clean and keep warm and safe. It should not have too many steps and stairs. It is an advantage if family, friends, shops, a post office, buses and recreational facilities are nearby.

Elderly people may like to live with their children or other relatives where they have the company of the family. If they can have a room of their own with some of their furniture and possessions, they can have some privacy and independence without feeling alone.

Flats, bungalows and homes are provided by local authorities and some voluntary organizations. They are usually specially built or adapted for the elderly. Some of these are 'sheltered', each room or flat being self-contained but with a warden who can easily be called if required by means of a bell. Sometimes these homes have a dining-room where there is an opportunity to meet and have the company of others in a similar age group.

Financial help and welfare

Financial help of various kinds is available. This is not 'charity' but a right, because of taxes and contributions paid during your working life and still paid on goods you buy. As well as the basic retirement pension, help may be given with rent, rates, heating costs, and maintenance and insurance of the house. Many local authorities allow reduced fares or free travel to older people. Shops sometimes reduce prices of hairdressing, dry-cleaning, shoe repairs and cinema tickets.

General advice about any kind of help is available through the Social Services department, the Social Security office, the Citizens' Advice Bureau or voluntary organizations such as 'Help the Aged'. The different kinds of help may include Meals-on-Wheels, home helps, chiropodist visits, help to visit a dentist or optician, social activities such as Over 60s clubs, lunch clubs, outings and holidays.

Health

Regular checks at the optician's and good lighting both help to prevent accidents and keep up interests and hobbies. Deafness may develop slowly, leading to a feeling of being cut off from conversations and other people. Hearing aids are free from the N.H.S. These may have extensions for television or radio. Good teeth or dentures are important for good eating and digestion. If feet are painful exercise will be reduced and it will be more difficult to keep up outside interests. Warmth is important. Older people are more likely to feel the cold if they are less active. Heating should be good, easy to manage and safe. A good diet, light, warm and easily washable clothes and bedding, woollen socks, knee caps and gloves all help in keeping warm. Pure wool is usually the warmest fibre for clothing and blankets.

Questions

1 **Describe the reasons why elderly people often have a poor diet and how they can be helped to overcome this.**
2 **What precautions could you take in your home to prevent falls?**
3 **How can older people be helped by their families to keep as fit and healthy as possible?**

Simple first aid

A knowledge of simple first aid is very useful in treating the minor accidents which can occur at any time in the home. Prompt and correct treatment can often prevent the need for further treatment later on. If the accident is more serious, medical help should be sought at once, by taking the patient to the casualty department of a hospital or by ringing for an ambulance or doctor.

First aid box

Every home should have a box of basic first aid equipment which is easily available when needed and yet is out of the reach of children. It should contain the following items:

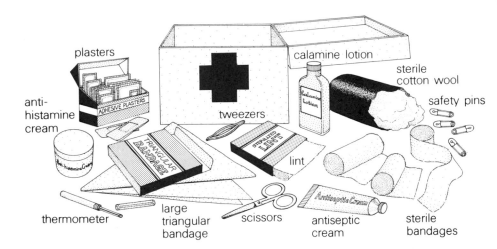

Simple treatments

1   *Small cuts* – Clean the wound with cool, running water, dry the skin with cotton wool and cover with a clean dressing.

2   *Minor burns and scalds* – Put under cool running water to reduce the heat and relieve the pain. Dry carefully and cover loosely with a clean, dry dressing. Never cover with fat, ointments or creams.

3   *Extensive burns and scalds* – Place gently in cool running water and keep immersed for at least ten minutes. Cover loosely with a clean, dry cloth and send for medical help at once.

4   *Fainting* – If someone feels faint, get them near fresh air and give them a drink of water. Put the head between the knees so that blood can reach the brain. If someone faints, keep them lying flat. Raise the legs slightly above the level of the head. Do not make them sit up or move too soon. Loosen any clothing which is tight round the neck, chest or waist.

5   *Nosebleeds* – Tilt the head slightly forward to prevent any blood being swallowed. Gently but firmly squeeze the nostrils. Breathing should be through the mouth.

6   *Insect bites or stings* – Remove the sting with tweezers. Relieve the pain with anti-histamine cream if you have it, or use a bicarbonate of soda solution (or saliva) for bees and other insects. For wasp stings, apply vinegar. Remember – 'Bicarb for bees, Winegar for wasps.'

7   *Dog bites* – If the skin has been cut, cover with a clean dressing and go to a hospital or doctor for injections against rabies and tetanus. Try to find out who owns the dog, so that it can be examined for disease.

8   *Poisoning* – Get medical help as soon as possible. Keep the poison so that it can be identified and keep any vomit. Treatment varies with the type of poison – if there are red marks around the mouth and lips, which suggest a strong corrosive poison, do not try to make the patient sick but give him large amounts of milk to drink (or water if no milk is available).

9   *Shock* is a physical state likely to follow any accident and can be more serious than the injury itself. If you think there may be a fracture or internal bleeding do not attempt to move the patient. Otherwise lay him down, make him comfortable and reassure him. Do not put on extra clothing or rugs and do not give any drinks.

Home nursing

Most people find they have to look after a sick person at home at some time. Following these general rules will help the patient to recover.

1   Follow carefully all the doctor's instructions about diet, pills and general care. Make a written note if necessary to help you remember.
2   Give all pills and medicines in the right amounts and at the right time.
3   Keep the patient calm and quiet. Do not allow too many visitors at first.
4   Keep the room clean, tidy, well ventilated and warm.
5   Put a paper bag for rubbish where the patient can reach it easily. It can easily and hygienically be disposed of later.
6   Keep the bed clean and neat and the pillows fluffed up.
7   Wash the patient regularly. Brush teeth and comb hair. Provide frequent changes of pyjamas or night-clothes.
8   Provide plenty of fresh water to drink.
9   Make sure the patient can call you if required by providing a small bell.
10   As the patient recovers, provide suitable amusement, with a radio, books, toys or magazines. Food is important to help recovery. Doctors' instructions about diet must be followed. Provide small meals at regular times. Serve them on a tray laid attractively with a tray cloth, perhaps with a posy of flowers. Foods should be easily digestible – for example, fish, chicken, and milk puddings. Avoid spicy foods, fried foods, pork and bacon, pickles, vinegary foods, rich cakes and pastries. All food must be scrupulously clean and fresh.

Questions
1   **What items should be kept in a first aid box at home?**
2   **What five minor accidents do you think you are most likely to have to deal with? Describe how you would treat each one.**
3   **Describe the occasions when you would call for medical help at once.**
4   **What are the rules for home nursing?**
5   **What special care should you take when providing the patient's meals?**

Personal hygiene

Care of the skin

A good standard of personal hygiene helps us to resist infection and to stay healthy. Everyone should follow these normal rules of hygiene and should encourage others to do the same.

1   Hands should be washed frequently, using warm water and soap, particularly after going to the toilet and before eating meals. In our daily lives we are always touching things handled by other people, such as money, door-handles, pets, the seats of buses or trains. These can all carry tiny organisms which are transferred on to our hands and then to our food and mouths and in this way bring infection into our bodies.

2   Skin should be washed regularly to remove sweat. The easiest way to do this is by having a shower or bath every day. If this is not possible then thorough washing with soap and warm water is just as good. It is essential to wash well under the arms every day to prevent the unpleasant smell caused by stale perspiration (sweat). Some people sweat more freely than others. They should avoid wearing nylon, polyester or other non-absorbent materials next to the skin, as this will feel uncomfortable and could cause an unpleasant smell which will be difficult to get rid of from clothes.

3   The use of <u>deodorants</u> and <u>anti-perspirants</u> can help. They should be applied to skin which is cool and clean. They work more efficiently if the hair under the arms is removed, either with a razor or with a special depilatory cream. Deodorants may simply prevent the perspiration from developing an unpleasant odour, whereas anti-perspirants prevent perspiration being produced in the part of the skin where they are applied. They can be bought as aerosol sprays, sticks, roll-on liquids or creams and may vary as to how well they work for an individual person. Some people naturally perspire more than others. They may find roll-on lotions or creams work better for them.

4   Underclothing should be clean and changed often. Cotton underwear is best and most comfortable as it is absorbent and so can soak up sweat from the surface of the skin.

Acne

Acne is quite common in teenagers, when oil-producing glands in the skin become very active. The pores become blocked by excessive grease and bacteria multiply in the grease, producing poisons which irritate the skin and cause the characteristic blemishes or marks.

What you can do to help control acne

1   Wash your skin frequently with soap and warm water to remove grease.
2   Use clean, well-washed hands to wash your face, not a flannel or sponge which may harbour bacteria.
3   A mild antiseptic soap may be helpful.
4   Cut greasy foods out of your diet – foods such as pastry, fried foods, cream, chocolate and pork.
5   Eat plenty of fresh fruit and vegetables and drink plenty of water.
6   Do not put greasy make-up or creams on your face.
7   Your doctor may prescribe a preparation to help clear your skin.

The care of your hair

1   Wash your hair as often as necessary to keep it clean and free from grease.
2   Brushing will smooth the hair and keep it shiny.
3   Wash your brush and comb regularly to remove grease, dead skin and dust.
4   A good diet helps to keep your hair in good condition – plenty of fresh fruit and vegetables and protein foods, but not too much greasy food.
5   Treat your hair with consideration. Do not use chemical bleaches, colourants, 'perm' lotions, sprays and so on too often. Ask the advice of a qualified hairdresser about cutting, conditioning, or colouring your hair and avoid drastic 'do-it-yourself' changes or treatments.
6   Do not use other people's combs. Dandruff is easily passed from one person to another. Like acne, it can occur when the sebaceous (oil-producing) glands of the skin are too active. It is best to ask your doctor for a special treatment shampoo.

Questions

1   **Why should we try to develop good standards of hygiene in ourselves and in our families?**
2   **What habits of personal hygiene would you encourage in a young child you were looking after?**
3   **What are the advantages of wearing cotton clothes next to the skin?**
4   **List all the advice you could give to someone who suffered from excessive perspiration.**
5   **What encouragement and advice could you offer to a friend who has acne?**
6   **How should you care for your hair?**

Caring for your teeth

We would all like to have perfect, strong teeth for the sake of our health, our appearance and our comfort. Decayed teeth can lead to pain, general ill-health, gum disease and digestive disorders as well as the loss of your teeth at an early age. There is a great deal you can do to keep your teeth in good condition.

Eating the right foods

1   The right kinds of food are all-important. For the teeth to grow and develop properly you need a good supply of calcium, phosphorus and vitamins D, C and A. This means you should have plenty of the foods which contain them, including milk, cheese, eggs, fresh fruit and vegetables.

2   Crisp, crunchy foods which need chewing and biting – such as apples, crusty bread, celery, raw carrots and nuts – are good, as they encourage the supply of blood to the teeth and gums and they help to keep the teeth clean.

3   Sweet, sticky foods are responsible for a large proportion of dental decay. Avoid these foods as much as you can, especially between meals. If you must eat sweets, eat them after a meal, then brush your teeth. It is especially harmful to leave a sweet, sticky layer of food in your mouth for long periods. The bacteria which normally live there act on this layer, forming a sticky substance called plaque on and around the teeth. The bacteria then produce an acid which begins to dissolve the hard enamel surface of the teeth and so they start to decay. If you brush your teeth thoroughly straight after eating sweet foods then this will not happen.

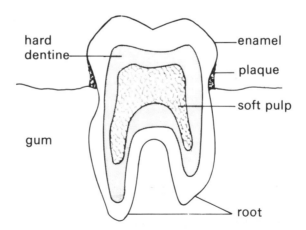

Brushing your teeth

Regular brushing is important. Try to brush your teeth after every meal and do not eat between meals, especially sweet foods. If you cannot brush after every meal, brush at least twice a day, after breakfast and before going to bed. Never go to bed without brushing your teeth. Think about all the hours the bacteria will have undisturbed to set about causing your teeth to decay!

Use a fluoride toothpaste – it helps reduce decay in both adults' and children's teeth. Brush your teeth correctly, from the gum to the cutting edge of the teeth. Do not brush the gum <u>away</u> from the teeth or you will cause infection to enter between the gum and the teeth.

Have regular checks at the dentist at six-monthly intervals. He can check any decay before it gets too bad. He can also apply fluoride treatment to the teeth which helps prevent decay for several months. Another new treatment, which can protect the teeth against decay for several years, involves coating some surfaces of the teeth with a thin, plastic film.

Fluoride

Where the mineral fluoride occurs naturally in drinking water, it has been found that children suffer much less tooth decay than in those areas where there is none. Because of this, it has been suggested that all water supplies in this country should have fluoride added to them to make up a level of one part of fluoride to one million parts of water. Other people consider that it would be wrong to force this measure upon everyone, regardless of whether they want it or not. Too much fluoride in the water can cause mottling of the teeth.

Care of children's teeth

If you are looking after children you have a particular responsibility to help them look after their teeth.

1 Do not let them eat sweets or sweet foods between meals. Never use sweets to bribe them 'to be good', or 'to keep them quiet'. You are doing them much more harm than good in the long run.
2 Encourage them to enjoy crisp, crunchy and savoury foods rather than sweet ones.
3 Never give a baby a dummy dipped in undiluted fruit syrup.
4 Teach children to be 'grown up' and brush their teeth at an early age. Eighteen months is not too young to start. You can buy small size tooth brushes, some of which have pictures of nursery characters on them.
5 Take them for a first visit to the dentist at the age of three or four, when they will enjoy looking around. Be careful not to put the idea into their heads that going to the dentist has to be an unpleasant experience!

Questions
1 **Name five nutrients which are needed for the development of healthy teeth.**
2 **Why should you eat plenty of crisp, fibrous foods?**
3 **Explain how teeth start to decay and draw a diagram showing the structure of a tooth.**
4 **List four important points to remember about brushing your teeth.**
5 **How often should you go to the dentist for a check-up?**
6 **Explain the argument in favour of adding fluoride to drinking water.**
7 **Give as many different reasons as you can to explain why it is unwise to give children sweets every time they ask for them.**

Further work on chapter 8

1   You usually babysit for your two-year-old brother if your parents go out. One evening you can't baby-sit as you are going out yourself. Three different friends of yours have offered to help. How would you decide which of them to choose and what would he/she would need to know before you went out?

2   Your grandfather lives alone and is finding it more and more difficult to cope on his own. What possible solutions and problems can your family consider?

3   A friend of yours is young, unmarried, and pregnant. Can you suggest any ways in which she could look for support and advice?

4   Most of your friends, with various skin types and colouring, are interested in caring for their skin, but can't afford a lot of expensive products. What can you find out about the basic rules of good skin care?

5   What can you find out about facilities in your area for either elderly people, handicapped or disabled people, or pre-school-age children?

Sources of further information

Help The Aged Education Department, PO Box 460, St James's Walk, London EC1R 0BE have many booklets and workcards.

Community Service Volunteers (address on page 26) has information, role-play games, worksheets, etc. on the family, community life, physical disability, homelessness among young people, etc.

Dr Barnado's (PAO), Tanners Lane, Barkingside, Essex IG6 1QG.

Films and videos
Subjects covered include social problems and support services, family life, disabilities, child care, pregnancy, health and skin care. Send a stamped, addressed envelope for full list.

EFVA National Audio Visual Aids Library (address on page 52).
Concord Film Council Ltd . (address on page 52).

Oxford Educational Resources, 197 Botley Road, Oxford OX2 OHE.

CFL Vision (address on page 168).

Books
All about children by Dorothy Baldwin, Oxford University Press.

All about health by Dorothy Baldwin, Oxford University Press.

Consumer's Guide to the British Social Services by P. Willmot, Pelican.

Chapter 9

Feeding the family

Shopping for food

When you are working out your family budget, you will decide how much you can spend on food. Try to spend the full amount actually <u>on</u> food; personal spending money for items like magazines, tights, cosmetics or sweets should be kept in a separate purse. Money spent on food is money well spent on your family's good health. There are many ways in which you can make sensible economies without cutting down on the nutritional value of your food.

Sensible ways to save money

1   Plan a week's meals in advance and you will be able to work out exactly how much you need to buy.

2   Make a shopping list of the things you need. Do not stick to it too strictly if there are any good offers which would be really useful to you.

3   Look out for 'special offers', but be careful. Ask yourself, is the article something you would have bought anyway? Do you really need it? Is it really much cheaper?

4   Get to know the usual prices of goods, then you will know whether a special offer is really much cheaper.

5   Do not go shopping too often. If you do your main shopping once a week, you may only need to go shopping again for fresh meat and bread and you will avoid the temptations of buying things you can really do without.

6   You can 'shop around', as costs for the same foods will vary from one shop to another. Whether you will want to do this will depend on the time and energy you have to spare.

7   Buy fruit and vegetables when they are in season as they will be cheap, plentiful and good – and you can find out just by looking carefully at the greengrocers. Cheaper fruit and vegetables are as good for you as more expensive ones. Cabbage, turnips and carrots, for example, are as good as cauliflower, mushrooms and peppers. If you live near a market you may find their fruit and vegetables are really fresh and quite a lot cheaper.

Look for fruit for making your own jams and marmalade – it will taste good and can be cheaper. Plum jam (late summer), rhubarb and ginger jam (early summer), blackberry and apply jelly (autumn) and marmalade are all cheap to make and delicious to eat.

8   Know which kinds of meat are cheaper. There are plenty of cookery books to give you ideas for appetizing meals using cheaper cuts of meat. Meat is usually cheaper because it is tougher or has more fat or bone, so you will have to consider whether or not it will be a better buy. Planning meals ahead will give you time to prepare and cook. A pressure cooker or a slow cooker is very good for tenderizing tougher cuts of meat. Cooking stews or casseroles with plenty of vegetables, or adding stuffing, rice, dumplings and so on all help meat to go further.

Use eggs, cheese, nuts, beans, or soya protein to make a main dish sometimes, as a substitute for meat.

9   Look for cheaper fish – mackerel and herring are cheap, as are tinned pilchards, and they are all good for you. Try a cheaper white fish such as coley or rock salmon. Cook them with a sauce, fry them, make a fish pie or fish cakes for a nutritious meal.

10   Home-made bread, cakes, scones and biscuits can be cheaper than bought ones and usually taste much better. Although it can take a lot of time, many people enjoy baking and nearly everyone enjoys eating home-baked food! Choose recipes carefully if you are trying to save money, otherwise it can be expensive. Remember also that cakes and pastries are a luxury rather than a necessity and that too many are not good for you or your figure.

11   If you have a freezer you can freeze fresh fruit and vegetables from your garden or when they are cheap to buy. (See page 116.) Meat, fish and vegetables from frozen food centres are often cheaper than fresh produce. You do not have to own a freezer to take advantage of their lower prices.

12   The most important thing to remember when trying to save on food bills is to spend your money on the foods which are best for you. Buy protein foods (meat, fish, milk, eggs and cheese), bread, fruit, vegetables and cereals. You can safely cut down on pastry, biscuits, cakes, chocolate, tinned fruit, cream, fruit squashes and crisps, foods which you may enjoy but are probably better without anyway.

Questions

1   **What are the advantages and disadvantages of making a shopping list and sticking to it?**
2   **What are the disadvantages of shopping daily?**
3   **What should you consider before buying 'special offers'?**
4   **How can you give your family plenty of fruit and vegetables without spending too much money?**
5   **Is it always economical to buy cheaper cuts of meat? Why?**
6   **If you were trying to save money, what foods would you (a) try to include in meals, and (b) feel you could safely cut down on?**

Food additives

Food additives are substances added to food in small quantities while it is being prepared for sale. If you make a habit of reading the labels on food packets you will soon realize that they are very widely used. They are added for one of two main reasons:

1 to prevent food going 'off'
2 to try to improve its colour, texture, or flavour.

Why they are so widely used

1 *To prevent food going off* In its natural state, food decays and goes 'off' fairly quickly. In this country most of us live in towns and cities quite a long way from where food is grown or produced. To keep it fresh until we can eat it, much of it is preserved by chilling, freezing, canning, packaging, or adding preservatives. The present vast range of reasonably priced foods on our supermarket shelves would not be available without preserved and processed foods.

2 *To try to improve its colour, texture, or flavour* Nowadays people expect a lot of the food they eat to be prepared and cooked in the factory, so that it is ready to eat. On the whole they spend less time preparing fresh ingredients at home and buy food in packets, jars, cans, or frozen. Nearly all foods are available like this – meat dishes, soups, vegetables, bread, cakes, biscuits, jams, sauces, and so on. For example, instead of spending time making soup by peeling, washing, cutting, and cooking fresh vegetables we may want to pour boiling water on to a packet mix and have the soup ready in minutes. Instead of making a cake with sugar, butter, eggs, and flour we may go to the supermarket for a cake in a packet that was made weeks ago and is kept fresh by additives.

When these foods are cooked in the factory and put into jars, cartons, tins, and so on, the natural colour, flavour, and texture is often altered, so additives are used to try to improve them in these respects. (See pages 204–5.)

Some possible effects of additives

Most people want to know whether additives are harmful or not. There is no simple answer to this question. The chemicals used can be of very different kinds. Some of them are used very widely, others are used very little. Some of them are used in tiny amounts but in many different foods and so consumption of them may be quite high. It is thought that some additives result in hyperactivity in children and allergic reactions in adults and children. Hyperactive children tend to be aggressive, to sleep very little, and to find it hard to sit still or concentrate. The same additives which can cause this hyperactivity in children can also produce allergic reactions such as migraine and skin rashes, especially in people who are allergic to aspirin. At the same time, many more people have allergic reactions to 'natural' foods like milk, cheese, eggs, strawberries, or shellfish.

Additives have to be tested to see whether they might cause these or other effects. But it is not easy to decide what effects they might have over a longer period, nor to know how much or how little of a substance may be considered 'safe' or 'harmful'. Not everyone reacts in the same way to the same additives.

ARE:
cake, Chocolate
vice cake and

3, York, YO1 1FS

INGREDIENTS: Cane Syrup, Flour, Animal Fat and Vegetable Oil, Sugar, Water, Whole Egg, Sorbitol (E420), Soya Flour, Fat Reduced Cocoa Powder, Cocoa Mass, Raising Agent (Sodium Bicarbonate), Salt, Dried Glucose Syrup, Gelling Agent (E401), Skimmed Milk Powder, Colour (E150), Whey Powder, Flavouring, Preservative (E202), Cornflour, Stabiliser (E412), Citric Acid (E330).

BEST BEFORE

E'S

colate

47p

16 12 85D

FREE

There are hundreds of additives on the 'permitted' list. Occasionally one is banned from use when there is reason to believe that it may be harmful. For example, Brown FK (for kippers) – E145 – may not be permitted for use much longer as it is suspected of being a cause of cancer. E102 – tartrazine – may also be banned as it is connected with hyperactivity and allergic reactions. It is very widely used at present as a yellow colouring.

Empty the contents of one of these sachets into a cup or mug. Then just add ⅓ pint (approx) of boiling water and stir well.

Ingredients: Modified Starch, Dried Glucose Syrup, Vegetable Fat, Salt, Flavour Enhancers 621, 635, Dried Chicken, Caseinates, Flavourings, Dried Onion, Acidity Regulator E340, Spices, Emulsifiers E471, E472(b), Herbs, Colours E150, E102, Antioxidants E320, E310.

Co-operative Wholesale Society Ltd., New Century House, Manchester

Additives in our daily diet

Overall it seems sensible to plan our daily meals around fresh, unprocessed foods as far as possible, and to keep the number of processed foods high in additives to a minimum.

Questions

1 **What are food additives?**
2 **What are the main reasons for the use of additives?**
3 **What kinds of foods tend to contain a lot of additives?**
4 **How are some children and adults affected by additives?**
5 **How do you feel about additives in your own diet? Would you feel the same if you were choosing food for your own children?**

Control of additives

The use of additives is controlled by the Food Act of 1984 which forbids the addition to food or drink of any substance which may be harmful to health. Under E.E.C. Food Labelling Regulations there must be information on food packets about the purpose of the additive and its name or agreed number. An 'E' in front of a number means that the food has been tested and is permitted for use throughout the E.E.C. Additives without the 'E' in front have the approval of the British Government but not the E.E.C.

For example, the mousse packet below includes on its ingredients list 'colours E122, E102, E142, E160a.' The soup packet on the previous page contains emulsifiers E471 and E472b.

You can send for a leaflet called 'Look at the Label' (see page 210) which lists the additives and their numbers and explains what they are used for.

Types of additive

They may be grouped into four main types, according to the purpose for which they are used.

1   *Additives to preserve food or improve its keeping qualities*

    This group includes:

    a   Preservatives – E200 numbers. These prevent food being spoiled by bacteria, mould, or yeasts, e.g. E202 Potassium sorbate.
    b   Anti-oxidants – E300 numbers. These prevent fats and oils from going rancid. You will often see them on snack foods like crisps which have been fried in oil, as well as on lard and margarine packets. Examples are E320 butylated hydroxyanisole (BHA), E321 Butylated hydroxytoluene (BHT).

2   *Additives to improve the texture and consistency of foods*

    This group includes:

    a   Emulsifiers, thickeners, and gelling agents – E400 numbers. They may, for example, stop foods like salad cream or instant dessert whips from dividing into separate layers, or make sure that jam 'gels' or sets. This group also includes humectants to keep foods soft and prevent them going dry (often used in bought cakes). They include sorbitol (E420) and glycerol (E422) which is found in cake icing.
    b   Anti-caking agents E551 to E572. They prevent powders or salt from sticking or caking in the packet, e.g. calcium silicate E552 is added to icing sugar to stop it going lumpy in the packet.

3 *Additives used to alter the appearance or taste of food or drink* This group includes colours, flavourings, and sweeteners.

   a Colours:

Yellows	E100s and E110s
Reds	E120s
Blues	E130s
Green	E140s
Browns and blacks	E150s

      E160s are all natural colourants rather than artificial ones. Some food manufacturers are changing to the use of these natural colours because some of the synthetic ones are suspected of having harmful effects.

      E170s are metal and mineral colourings.

    Examples of colourings used are:

      E102 tartrazine, a yellow widely used at present

      E142 Green S (Acid Brilliant Green BS or Lissamine Green)

      E160a carotene, a natural yellow colour often used in margarine

      E174, the silver in edible cake decorations.

All these foods contain artificial colourings

   b *Flavours* and flavour enhancers, the E600 numbers. For example, E621 monosodium glutamate, is used to bring out flavour in foods.

   c *Sweeteners.* These do not have E numbers but there is a list of artificial sweeteners, including saccharin and aspartame, which are permitted in the U.K.

4 Additives for miscellaneous purposes include anti-foaming agents to prevent pineapple juice from frothing too much, flour improvers, acids, raising agents, and glazing agents to give a shine to confectionery.

Questions

1 **What are the four main purposes of putting additives in foods?**
2 **Which are the numbers for 'natural' food colourings?**
3 **What does it tell you if a number has no 'E' in front of it?**
4 **Why is a sliced wrapped loaf more likely to stay fresh much longer than one from a local bakery? Which costs more? Which tastes better?**

Food labelling

Now that food manufacturers have to list all the ingredients and additives on packet labels it is easier to see what is being offered and to decide whether we want to buy. More people are becoming interested in following the recommendations for a healthy diet – eating more fibre, less sugar, less fat, less salt. Many people, too, want to cut out food with a lot of additives. Because of this, food manufacturers may advertise their products as being 'low in fat',' 'sugar-free', 'high in fibre', or 'free from artificial colours or preservatives'. This is a useful guide, but at the same time you may find that though foods are 'good' in one way they are not so good in another. For example, a bran breakfast cereal may be 'good' in that it is high in fibre but it could well have a lot of extra sugar. A fruit drink may be advertised as 'sugar-free' but may contain a lot of artificial colours and sweeteners. If you start to read food labels you will pick up a lot of information and will be able to make a more informed choice about what you eat.

Food labelling in Britain

Food labelling in Britain is controlled by E.E.C. regulations which came into effect in 1983. The regulations are intended to give shoppers useful information and to update and improve the law. As so much of the food we eat is hidden away inside packets, tins, and cartons, good labelling is particularly important.

The label must give certain information, and it must be easy to see, to read, and to understand. It must tell you the following:

1. The name of the food.
2. The ingredients.
3. The instructions for use.
4. The datemark.
5. Storage instructions.
6. Net quantity i.e. without packaging.
7. Name and address of manufacturer or packer.
8. Place of origin.
9. Special claims.

Some foods are exempt from these regulations and have their own rules, including milk, honey, hens' eggs, sugar, chocolate, and coffee.

1. *The name of the food* This must be shown on the label and must not mislead the customer. For example, cartons of orange juice can only be called 'juice' if they are pure juice. If they are a mixture of different ingredients which taste of orange, then they may only be called orange 'drink'.

2. *The ingredients* Labels on pre-packed food must show a complete list of ingredients, in descending order of weight (heaviest first). That means that the ingredient there is most of is shown first. In this way you can tell, for instance, if what is called a 'beef curry with rice' is in fact nearly all rice, soya, and flavouring with very little beef in it. Any food additives must be included in the list. (See previous page.)

3. *The instructions for use* These must be shown if it is not obvious what to do.

Ingredients:-
Wholemeal Flour,
Vegetable Fat and
Hydrogenated
Vegetable Fat,
Sugar, Cane Syrup,
Raising Agents
(Sodium Bicarbonate,
Tartaric Acid, Ammonium
Bicarbonate), Salt.

NO ARTIFICIAL COLOURS OR FLAVOURS

NUTRITION INFORMATION

	TYPICAL COMPOSITION	
	per biscuit	per 100 g
Energy	257 kJ / 61 kcal	2055 kJ / 488 kcal
Protein	1·0 g	7·7 g
Carbohydrate	9·3 g	74·1 g
Fat	2·5 g	20·0 g

STORE IN A COOL DRY PLACE AWAY FROM STRONG LI
MADE IN GREAT BRITAIN BY McVITIE'S. P.O. BOX 63, YORK

CONSUMER CARE

NUTRITION INFORMATION
100 GRAMS OF THIS PRODUCT
TYPICALLY PROVIDES:

5.1 grams of Protein	MEDIUM
14.3 grams of Carbohydrate	HIGH
0.2 grams of Fat	LOW
5.4 grams of Dietary Fibre	HIGH
Energy Value (Calories)	324 kJ (76 kcal)

INGREDIENTS
Beans, Water, Tomato Puree, Sugar,
Salt, Modified Starch, Spices.

TO SERVE
Empty contents into a saucepan and
heat gently until thoroughly warm.

PRODUCED IN GREAT BRITAIN

250 μg
2.8 μg
1.7 μg
6.7 mg

1.8 mg

R ADDED

UTRI-GRAIN come
ingredients.
icial flavours
urs.

y fall below the high
ss's, please send the
sumer Services,
reat Britain Limited,
M32 8RA.
of Ireland Limited,
nshaugh, Dublin 17.
We will refund postage.
are not affected.

© 1986/1987 KELLOGG COMPANY
® Trademarks Registered
TM—Trademarks
Made in U.K.

This package contains at least 12 of the above
servings and is sold by weight, not volume.
Some settling of contents may have occurred
during transit.

THE WINDMILL BAKERY

6 WHOLEMEAL SCOTCH ROLLS
made from 100% wholemeal flour

NO PRESERVATIVES

Freezing: Windmill
holemeal Scotch Rolls
are ideal for freezing.
Place in deep freeze on
day of purchase; use
within three months.

Quality Control Dept.
British Bakeries Ltd.
, Box 178, Alma Road
indsor, Berks SL4 3ST

SELL BY 26 JUN X84 49p

Eat within
1 day of
date shown

375 g

Carton No. 09 04 02/5

Ingredients: Wholemeal Flour, Water, Wheat Protein, Hydrogenated Vegetable Oil, Salt, Dried Glucose Syrup,
Yeast, Vinegar, Emulsifiers (E471, E472[e]), Soya Flour, Flour Improver: Ascorbic Acid (Vitamin C).

4   *The datemark* Under the 1983 regulations date-marking became compulsory for most foods. (Some of the exceptions are frozen foods, fresh bread and cakes, fresh fruit and vegetables, sugar, and food which will last over 18 months.

   The datemark is usually in the form 'best before' followed by the day, month, and year. Sometimes the day or year can be left out. The food should stay in peak condition as regards flavour, crispness, and so on up to the date shown.

   Perishable foods like cream or yogurt which should be eaten within a few days or weeks of packing may instead be marked by a 'sell-by' date. The label should also tell you that the contents should be eaten within so many days of buying and how you should store the food if it is to keep fresh for that time.

   Sometimes you can see food past its date being sold cheaply in shops. This is not illegal provided the food is fit for consumption and the customer realizes what is being offered.

5   *Storage instructions* are important if the datemarks are to apply, e.g. if you keep a packet of butter in a warm kitchen when it should be stored in the fridge you cannot expect it to keep fresh for the recommended time.

6   *Net quantity,* that is, without any packaging. This must be shown by weight or by volume of the packet or can. Eggs and breakfast cereals, such as Weetabix and Shredded Wheat need only state how many items are inside the packet.

7   *Name and address of manufacturer or packer* of the food must be shown because they are responsible for the original condition of the food.

8   *Place of origin* should be shown if it is likely to be other than what the buyer might have expected.

9   *Special claims* Some foods claim to be suitable for slimmers, babies, or diabetics, or to contain extra amounts of vitamins or minerals. Any claims like this must be backed up with clear factual information on the label. (For nutritional information see page 208.)

Labelling of eggs

The labels on egg boxes are designed to give you the following information:

The size of the egg by weight, numbered from 1 to 7. Size 1 is the largest.
The number of eggs inside – usually 6 or 12.
The quality of the eggs – class A or B.
The registered number of the packing station, with the country, the area, and the station number.
The date or week (from 1 to 52) they were packed.
The higher the week number the fresher the eggs. They may also or instead have a 'sell-by' date.
The packer's name and address.

Nutritional information on food labels

Some manufacturers, such as Birds Eye, Walls, Findus, and Weetabix provide nutritional information on their packets, though this is not needed by law. To be able to understand this information you need to have a little background information already, namely:

1 Food contains different nutrients such as protein, fat, carbohydrates, vitamins, minerals, and dietary fibre. (See *All about food* by Helen McGrath, Oxford University Press.)
2 Certain daily amounts are recommended for most people.
3 A certain number of daily calories is recommended too. This is of particular interest to people who want to lose weight on a calorie-controlled diet.
4 The general recommendations for healthy eating are: include plenty of fibre in your diet, and cut down on fats, sugar, and salt. Many people also want to avoid foods with a lot of additives.

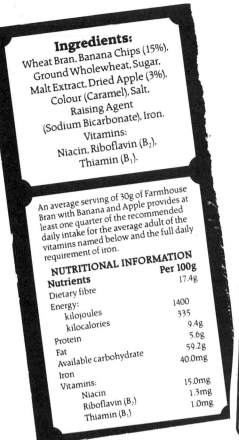

Ingredients:

Wheat Bran, Banana Chips (15%), Ground Wholewheat, Sugar, Malt Extract, Dried Apple (3%), Colour (Caramel), Salt, Raising Agent (Sodium Bicarbonate), Iron. Vitamins: Niacin, Riboflavin (B_2), Thiamin (B_1).

An average serving of 30g of Farmhouse Bran with Banana and Apple provides at least one quarter of the recommended daily intake for the average adult of the vitamins named below and the full daily requirement of iron.

NUTRITIONAL INFORMATION

Nutrients	Per 100g
Dietary fibre	17.4g
Energy:	
kilojoules	1400
kilocalories	335
Protein	9.4g
Fat	5.6g
Available carbohydrate	59.2g
Iron	40.0mg
Vitamins:	
Niacin	15.0mg
Riboflavin (B_2)	1.3mg
Thiamin (B_1)	1.0mg

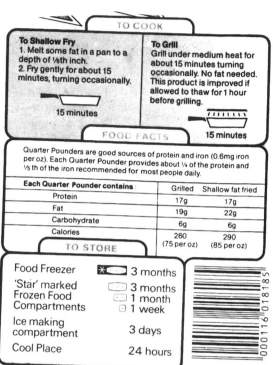

TO COOK

To Shallow Fry
1. Melt some fat in a pan to a depth of 1/8th inch.
2. Fry gently for about 15 minutes, turning occasionally.

15 minutes

To Grill
Grill under medium heat for about 15 minutes turning occasionally. No fat needed. This product is improved if allowed to thaw for 1 hour before grilling.

15 minutes

FOOD FACTS

Quarter Pounders are good sources of protein and iron (0.6mg iron per oz). Each Quarter Pounder provides about 1/4 of the protein and 1/5 th of the iron recommended for most people daily.

Each Quarter Pounder contains:	Grilled	Shallow fat fried
Protein	17g	17g
Fat	19g	22g
Carbohydrate	6g	6g
Calories	260 (75 per oz)	290 (85 per oz)

TO STORE

Food Freezer		3 months
'Star' marked Frozen Food Compartments		3 months
		1 month
		1 week
Ice making compartment		3 days
Cool Place		24 hours

Questions

1 **What basic information must be shown on all food packets?**
2 **If you saw a pizza for sale on its 'sell-by' date, marked at half price, would you think it was a good buy? Why?**
3 **What are the general guidelines for a normal healthy diet?**
4 **By studying the food packets above, see if you can work out the following information:**

   a **What method of cooking the beefburgers (Quarter Pounders) is best for someone on a calorie-controlled diet?**
   b **Which of these foods is the best source of iron?**
   c **What is the daily recommended amount of protein for most people?**
   d **Which of these foods is a good source of fibre?**
   e **What is the daily recommended intake of vitamin B_1, (thiamin)?**

Further work on chapter 9

1   Look in your food cupboard at home to see if the various food packets follow the Food Labelling Regulations on page 206. Choose any three packets or labels and check the necessary information for each one.

2   Find out which additives are most widely used in foods. Look at at least 10 food labels, list all the different additives, and note how many times each one appears. What are they used for and what do you think the food might be like without them? 'Look at the Label' (see below) tells you the chemical names of each additive, e.g. E464 = Hydroxypropylmethylcellulose!)

3   Keep a list of all the foods you actually eat in one day: breakfast, lunch, tea, other meals, and snacks. Write down all the additives in the foods.

4   Suggest meals and snacks you could eat during one day if you wanted to keep your intake of additives low.

5   Choose five foods your family buys every week. Look in the shops and see what is the lowest price you can find for each of them, and what is the highest. Work out the difference between the total of the five cheapest and the total of the five dearest prices. Taking your findings into account, do you think you should make any changes in the way your weekly shopping is done?

Sources of further information

The Health Education Council, 78 New Oxford St., London WC1A 1AH has leaflets on food packaging and labelling.

'Look at the Label', Ministry of Agriculture, Fisheries and Food, Willowburn Trading Estate, Alnwick, Northumberland NE66 2PF. This explains what labels on pre-packed food mean and gives a list of additives. They have a film/video of the same name, obtainable from CFL Vision.

Films and videos
These cover many aspects of food, diet, additives, wholefoods, etc. and are for hire or sale (ask for a list) from the following: CFL Vision (address on page 168); Concord Films Council (address on page 52); EFVA (address on page 52).

Books
E for Additives by Maurice Hanssen, Thorsons, Wellingborough.
All about food by Helen McGrath, Oxford University Press.

Computer software
'Food for the Family' and 'Eating for Health', BBC Microspecial Pack, simple level. Covers food choice, value for money, shopping.

Chapter 10

Work and leisure

Leaving school

Your last year at school is a good time to think about what you are going to do when you leave. You will probably have a <u>careers teacher</u> at school who will be able to advise you on everything related to jobs, training, suitable school subjects for certain jobs, any qualifications you might need, whether there are prospects of moving up to a better paid or more interesting job when you have some experience. The careers teacher may arrange for people from different kinds of jobs or occupations to come to the school to tell you about their kind of work. He/she may be able to arrange some work experience for you, so that you can see what it is like working in a particular kind of place.

Finding work

In many areas it is very difficult for young people and others to find a job. Most people want a job, perhaps because:

They like to have money, and the possibility of earning more as they get more experienced.

Being at home with nothing to do can seem like a holiday at first, but for most people it soon becomes boring and depressing.

They like to have the company of the people they work with.

They like to feel they are doing something useful.

The careers officer

Every Local Education Authority has a <u>careers officer</u> whose job it is to help school-leavers. He/she will have a talk with you and your parents in your last year at school. He/she will know what the employment situation in your area is like and will discuss with you what you would like to do, and what is likely to be available in the way of jobs, Youth Training Schemes, or courses at a College of Further Education. He/she will help you arrange this. You can also get in touch with him/her at the local Careers Office. The address will be in the phone book, under the name of your City or County Council's Education Department. Besides helping you find work or training he/she will help you sort out any problems which occur during your first year or two after leaving school.

Jobcentres

These are more for older school-leavers or for any other adults looking for work. In the Jobcentre there are cards on display describing different jobs that are available. If you see a job you think may be suitable you can get more details by asking at the desk. They can arrange an interview for you, sometimes straight away, so it is a good idea to go there suitably dressed and prepared.

Youth training schemes
If you cannot find a job or a Further Education course (see below) you will be offered a Y.T.S. place, for two years if you are 16, or one year if you are 17. As well as training on the job, you get suitable training in a college or training centre. You receive a certain amount of money per week and do not have to pay Income Tax or National Insurance. If you complete a course on a well run scheme you should gain experience, skills, and a certificate, all of which should be really useful to you when you look for a job.

Action for jobs
This is a booklet published by the Department of Employment/Manpower Services Commission, available free from any of their offices or from D.H.S.S. or Post Offices. It describes their many employment, training, and enterprise programmes, including help with starting to work for yourself, Community Programmes, Job Training Schemes, Job Search Schemes, and Job Splitting Schemes.

Colleges of Further Education
These offer a wide range of practical and vocational courses leading to qualifications given by the City and Guilds Institute, B/TEC (Business and Technician Education Council), the R.S.A. (Royal Society of Arts), and to the C.P.V.E. (Certificate of Pre-Vocational Education). These courses are usually closely linked to the jobs that are likely to be available in your area. You are allowed to study part-time for up to 21 hours a week without losing your right to Social Security benefit if you have been unemployed for three months or more.

Higher education
Courses at a higher level are run in Polytechnics and Universities. You need exam qualifications for entry, and your careers officer or teacher will be able to advise you.

Questions
1 **When should you start thinking about a career?**
2 **How can the careers teacher and careers officer help you?**
3 **How could you get in contact with the careers officer in your area?**
4 **How could you benefit from taking a Further Education course?**
5 **Explain the possible advantages of going on a Youth Training Scheme.**

Interviews

When you first apply for a job it will usually be by letter in response to an advertisement in the paper, or through the Careers Officer.

The employer will probably receive several letters, and using them as a guide he will select some of the applicants to come for an interview. You want your letter to be selected as one of the best written so that you will have an interview, so take care to write a good letter in your best handwriting.

Use plain, good quality writing paper without lines and write in your own handwriting. A fine felt-tipped pen, or a fountain pen, usually produces better writing than a ball-point pen.

A sample letter is shown below. The general pattern would be the same if you were applying for a place on a college course.

> 29, Middleton Avenue,
> Felling.
> FE3 4PQ
> June 15 1987
>
> Personnel Manager,
> Williams Stores,
> Felling.
>
> Dear Sir,
>
> I would like to apply for the position of Trainee Sales Assistant as described in the Felling Advertiser of June 14. I am very keen to begin a career in selling and feel that this would be a good opportunity for me to receive a sound training.
>
> I am 16 years old and leave Felling School in July this year. I expect to have six G.C.S.E. passes at good grades, including English, Maths and typing. I would be very pleased to come for an interview at any time.
>
> Yours faithfully
> T. A. Wilson.

Before you are offered a job or place in college, you will nearly always have to attend an interview. The impression you make can be very important in deciding whether or not you are offered the place.

Appearance

Take particular care with your appearance. You want to give your prospective employer a good impression and to look as though you will take your work seriously. You should try to look well groomed, neat and tidy, rather than way-out and extremely fashionable. Make sure that your shoes are well polished and your clothes well brushed and clean. Do not wear a lot of perfume, make-up or jewellery and keep your hair in a neat, tidy style.

Try to appear calm and confident even though you may be feeling nervous. If you are introduced to someone, smile and say 'Hello' or 'How do you do?' Be ready to shake hands if required.

A few days before the interview think about the questions you may be asked, and have some ideas ready. You may be asked why you want the job, or whether you would be prepared to study at afternoon or evening classes to improve your skill at the job.

The interview is the time for you to ask any questions you have, perhaps about the work involved, salary, prospects of promotion, training schemes, hours or holidays. These will show that you are interested in the job. Speak clearly and be polite and well-mannered, and let the employer see that you will be an asset to his or her staff!

Questions
1   **Why is it important to write your letter of application carefully?**
2   **What kind of paper and pen will give a good impression to a possible employer?**
3   **Write a letter similar to the one shown above, applying for a job you would like.**
4   **Write a letter to a college, enquiring about evening classes in a subject which interests you. You should address your letter to 'The Principal'.**
5   **You have been asked to go for an interview for a job in a department store or office. Describe how you would dress. List some of the clothes you would not wear on this occasion.**
    6Write down three of the questions which (a) you might be asked at the interview, and (b) you would ask about the job.

Voluntary work

Voluntary organizations exist to bring together those people needing help, perhaps children, the elderly, disabled, or homeless, with people who have the time and the wish to help them. Voluntary workers are not paid, but they have the satisfaction of knowing that they are helping people in their own community. People of all ages can offer their help for voluntary work. They may be young people still at school or older people who have retired from paid work or whose children have grown up, leaving them with time on their hands. They may be unemployed people who find it a useful and worthwhile way of spending their time. Doing voluntary work may even help unemployed people to get a paid job because it shows they have initiative and have spent their time in a useful way. They may also be able to get a reference from the organization to help them find work. (As long as you still sign on and are available for interviews, voluntary work will not affect benefit payments.)

There is always a need for people who can give free part-time help of any kind. If you feel you could offer your help but do not know whom to contact, get in touch with your County or Borough Council for Voluntary Service or the Citizens' Advice Bureau (addresses in the phone book), or write to Community Service Volunteers (address on page 26) or the Voluntary Service Opportunity Register.

The work they do

The voluntary organizations do valuable work in adding to and working with the state-provided services. They are usually experts in their own field, e.g. the N.S.P.C.C., Help The Aged, The British Red Cross Society, and have a detailed knowledge of the needs and difficulties of the people they help. Because of this they can bring pressure on the government to improve the law or grant extra resources in their own particular field. They also bring the attention of the public to the needs of particular groups, as do Shelter, for example, in their work for the homeless. Many of them are charities and do not cost the state any money because they raise their own funds.

Some voluntary organizations and their work

The N.S.P.C.C. (National Society For The Prevention of Cruelty To Children) looks after children in need, investigating reports of cruelty or neglect of children, trying to help and advise parents with difficulties, and bringing the interests of children to the attention of the government.

Shelter aims to help families who are homeless or who have any kind of housing problem. They try to bring pressure on the government to improve the position of the many people without a decent home.

Gingerbread provides support for one-parent families. It encourages people to set up self-help groups where those in similar situations can meet and give each other friendship and support. It also works for reforms in the law to improve the position of one-parent families.

Age Concern provides help and advice of many kinds for the elderly. Within local communities it provides day-centres where old people can meet, arranges visitors for those who are house-bound, provides transport where old people need it, meals-on-wheels, help in working out entitlement to state benefits and generally represents the interests of the elderly to the government.

The Samaritans operate a 24-hour service to answer phone calls. Anyone who feels distressed or unhappy can ring them and they will always listen sympathetically and in complete confidence. If you want, you can arrange a visit to talk to one of their counsellors.

Environment groups, such as Friends of The Earth, are always looking for help and support for different projects concerned with maintaining the quality of the environment.

Oxfam relies on voluntary help in its projects to raise money. Their charity shops, for example, are run by volunteers.

Local groups of all kinds are usually looking for helpers for local projects, perhaps to raise money for a local hospital, children's home, school, church, or youth centre.

Questions

1 **What are voluntary organizations?**
2 **Who may be likely to have spare time to do some voluntary work?**
3 **If you wanted to do some voluntary work, how would you get in touch with people needing your help?**
4 **Describe in your own words the work done by two voluntary organizations which you feel do really useful work.**

The community and you

A community is a group of people living in the same area. It includes everyone in that area: families, single people, old people, teenagers, children, and babies.

Most people in any neighbourhood can do something to contribute to the feeling of community spirit and friendliness in the area. This helps people feel settled and 'at home', and part of the place they live in. There are many things which can help this kind of feeling to develop, for example, the design of the houses and flats that people live in. If houses are grouped together so that people meet and get to know each other at their front doors then they are likely to develop friendly relationships with each other. Their children get to know each other and most of the parents know most of the children. This reduces the likelihood of vandalism and damage to property, keeping the neighbourhood looking tidy and well cared for. It helps too when most of the people have lived in the same place for a long time. When people move in and out of a neighbourhood without staying long, for example in an area where lots of students live in flats and bedsitters, it is difficult for people to build up stable relationships with their neighbours.

In many areas there are community centres where people living in the same neighbourhood can meet and take part in all kinds of activities. They provide a place and opportunity for people of all ages to meet others in the same circumstances as themselves, perhaps at a playgroup for parents and under-fives, social clubs for old people, keep-fit groups for anyone interested, and youth clubs and discos for young people.

Some communities have oganizations to help local people with problems. They could include Housing Advice Centres, the Citizens' Advice Bureau, Drop-in Centres for the unemployed, Residents' Associations, or Tenants' Associations.

Leisure

Leisure could be described as the time we spend doing the things we want to do, instead of the things we have got to do like going to work or school. A balance between work and leisure is good for most people. Leisure helps you relax from mentally or physically tiring work and to forget about it. It gives you time to mix with people and make friends. You can gain the satisfaction of doing something interesting, or learning or thinking about something new. You can get physical enjoyment from an energetic activity such as football, horse-riding, swimming, or disco-dancing.

What influences our leisure?

The way we spend our spare time is decided by several factors:

1 The amount of spare money we have. Even the cheapest of leisure activities can cost money in fares and entrance fees, and the cost of buying kit and equipment for sporting interests can be very high. Sometimes people receiving state benefit such as unemployment benefit can get reduced fares and entrance fees to places like swimming pools, evening classes, cinemas, leisure centres, and so on.
2 Whether you live in a town, a city, or the country, and what amenities there are (if any) such as youth clubs, snooker halls, skating rinks.
3 The kind of work you do. If you do heavy physical work you might just want to relax at home or in a club or pub in your spare time. If your job involves sitting at a desk all day you might feel like taking up an energetic sport like football.

Some ways in which people spend their leisure time

1 Talking to friends at home, in the street, in clubs or pubs.
2 Physical activities like football, weight-training, aerobics, dancing, swimming.
3 Interests such as reading, collecting things, playing music, conservation.
4 Day or evening classes at community centres, schools, or Colleges of Further Education, in all sorts of subjects from jewellery-making or car maintenance to learning a foreign language or how to cook.

Questions

1 **What helps a sense of community spirit to develop in a neighbourhood?**
2 **What kind of activities can be held in a community centre?**
3 **How do leisure activities benefit people who take part in them?**
4 **What influences people's choice of leisure activities?**
5 **List some leisure activities, putting first the ones which cost least and ending with those which are very expensive.**

Further work on chapter 10

1   You are in your last year at school and are looking for a job. Look at the 'Situations Vacant' column in your local newspaper. Note the different types of jobs advertised – in catering, engineering, shops, factories, hotels, transport, sales, and any others. Which category has most jobs? Select a job that you would like to apply for and prepare a letter of application for it. Discuss your letter with your teacher and see if either of you can improve upon it. Keep a copy to help you when you start looking for work seriously.

2   New neighbours have moved in next door to you and have asked about places in the neighbourhood where people can meet for entertainment, leisure, information, advice, and so on. What can you tell them?

3   While you are looking for a job after leaving school, you have decided to offer a few hours unpaid work a week to a local group. How could you go about arranging this?

4   Finding a job when you leave school can be a problem. Start to find out now what will be involved in looking for a job (or Further Education) in your area.

Sources of further information

Local papers, Jobcentres, and people you know can all be means of finding out about jobs.

Your local College of Further Education will give you details of all their courses, both for leisure, and for training and qualifications, which will help you find a job.

The local library often keeps a list of clubs and societies in your neighbourhood.

Community Service Volunteers (address on page 26) have information, slides, worksheets, etc. on various aspects of community work and explain how you can become involved.

Books
Things You Need To Know by Pen Keyte, Oxford University Press
Consumer's Guide to the British Social Services by P. Willmot, Pelican.

Index